Hong Kong English

D1613054

Dialects of English

Series Editors
Joan Beal (University of Sheffield)
Patrick Honeybone (University of Edinburgh)
April McMahon (University of Edinburgh)

Advisory Board
Laurie Bauer (Victoria University of Wellington)
Jenny Cheshire (Queen Mary, University of London)
Karen P. Corrigan (Newcastle University)
Heinz Giegerich (University of Edinburgh)
Peter L. Patrick (University of Essex)
Peter Trudgill (University of Fribourg, UEA, Agder UC, La Trobe
    University)
Walt Wolfram (North Carolina State University)

Volumes available in the series:
Robert McColl Millar, *Northern and Insular Scots*
David Deterding, *Singapore English*
Jennifer Hay, Margaret Maclagan and Elizabeth Gordon, *New Zealand English*
Pingali Sailaja, *Indian English*
Karen P. Corrigan, *Irish English, volume 1 – Northern Ireland*
Jane Setter, Cathy S. P. Wong and Brian H. S. Chan, *Hong Kong English*

Forthcoming titles include:
Bridget L. Anderson, *Smoky Mountain English*
Sandra Clarke, *Newfoundland and Labrador English*
Jeff Kallen, *Irish English, volume 2 – The Republic of Ireland*
Joan Beal, Lourdes Burbano Elizondo and Carmen Llamas, *Urban
    North-Eastern English: Tyneside to Teeside*

Hong Kong English

Jane Setter, Cathy S. P. Wong and Brian H. S. Chan

Edinburgh University Press

© Jane Setter, Cathy S. P. Wong and Brian H. S. Chan, 2010

Edinburgh University Press Ltd
22 George Square, Edinburgh

www.euppublishing.com

Reprinted 2012

Typeset in 10.5/12 Janson
by Servis Filmsetting Ltd, Stockport, Cheshire, and
printed and bound in Great Britain by
CPI Antony Rowe, Chippenham and Eastbourne

A CIP record for this book is available from the British Library

ISBN 978 0 7486 3595 5 (hardback)
ISBN 978 0 7486 3596 2 (paperback)

The right of Jane Setter, Cathy S. P. Wong and Brian H. S. Chan
to be identified as authors of this work
has been asserted in accordance with
the Copyright, Designs and Patents Act 1988.

Published with the support of the Edinburgh University Scholarly Publishing
Initiatives Fund.

Contents

Acknowledgements

First and foremost, we would like to acknowledge our debt to the five Hong Kong English speakers whose spoken data appear in this book, to Alois Heuboeck (the interviewer) and Iran M. Heuboeck for collecting the data and completing a first draft of the transcripts so diligently, and to the University of Reading for supporting the research for which the data were originally collected. We would also like to thank Vesna Stojanovik, Heike Pichler and Matt Moreland at the University of Reading for giving helpful comments on various sections of the manuscript, April McMahon for an instructive critique of the entire first draft, and Esmé Watson at Edinburgh University Press for keeping us on track throughout. Finally, thanks go to our colleagues and students, former and current, and our families, for their encouragement and support during the writing of this book.

1 Geography, demography and cultural factors

There is no doubt that Hong Kong is seen as one of the most excit-
ing cities in the world. The view across the harbour at night looking
towards the neon lights, a silhouette of a junk against the setting sun,
or the hubbub of lively business and commerce in a 24-hour city are
quintessential images conjured up in the mind when one thinks of this
exotic location. The self-portrait of Hong Kong as presented on the
official government internet website[1] describes it as 'a vibrant city, and
a major gateway to China'. Indeed, the geographic location of Hong
Kong has unequivocally placed it as an entry port to greater China.
The historical development of the city as well as the cultural composi-
tion of its population have provided the dynamics necessary for Hong
Kong to thrive as a cosmopolitan urban centre in the Pearl River Delta
region.

Hong Kong, a Special Administrative Region (SAR) of the People's
Republic of China (PRC), is located adjacent to the Pearl River Delta,
in the south-eastern region of China's Guangdong province, facing
the South China Sea. Contrary to popular belief, Hong Kong is not
just a single island territory comprising a built-up urban cityscape, but
includes three major parts: Hong Kong Island, the Kowloon Peninsula
and the New Territories. It is replete with country parks, sandy beaches
and outlying islands large and small. Along the northern part of the
New Territories is the border between Hong Kong and China. South
of the New Territories is Boundary Street, which used to mark the
boundary between Kowloon and the New Territories. The Kowloon
Peninsula extends into the famous Victoria Harbour, one of the world's
most renowned deep-water harbours. Across Victoria Harbour is Hong
Kong Island. In addition to these three major administrative regions,
there are 262 outlying islands within Hong Kong, the largest of which is
Lantau Island. Until July 1998, travellers used to arrive at Kai Tak, an
airport directly in the midst of the built-up region of Kowloon, flying
past tower blocks close enough to see people eating their midday meals

1

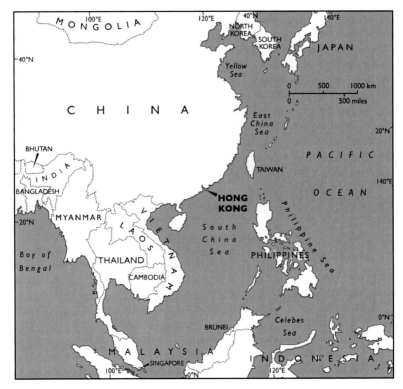

Figure 1.1 The Asia-Pacific region

or watching evening television; now the airport is at Chek Lap Kok
on Lantau Island, requiring a 30-minute journey through countryside,
over bridges and past towns and villages to reach the busy commercial
areas.

The total area of the Hong Kong SAR is 1,104km² (425 square miles).
The New Territories is the largest region, taking up 952km² (368 square
miles), and most of it consists of rural areas. Figure 1.1 shows Hong
Kong in relation to its neighbours, where the larger-scale Figure 1.2
shows the detail of Hong Kong itself. The Pearl River Delta is just off
this map, to the north-west.[2]

At the end of 2008, according to the provisional statistics available
at the Hong Kong Census and Statistics Department (www.gov.hk/en/
about/abouthk/facts.htm), Hong Kong's population had just reached 7
million, with slightly more females (3.7 million) than males (3.3 million).
The population growth stands at a relatively low rate of 0.8 per cent.
The life expectancy of the average Hongkonger is quite high: 85.5 years

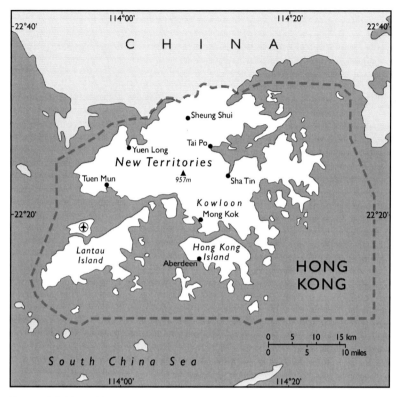

Figure 1.2 Hong Kong

of age for females and 79.4 for males. The average domestic household size is 3.0, indicating that the average family in Hong Kong is composed of a nuclear family: two parents plus one child. As in most developed countries, the citizens live longer while the birth rate is declining; Hong Kong is heading towards an ageing population.

Because of the small size of Hong Kong and its considerable population, the population density is 6,340 people per km². Hong Kong is one of the most densely populated cities in the world. Of the resident population, 95 per cent is ethnic Chinese, of whom 52 per cent have been educated to secondary school level, while 24 per cent have reached tertiary level education. Among the minority groups, Filipinos (1.6 per cent) and Indonesians (1.3 per cent) are the two largest; their presence is welcomed, as they are mainly employed as domestic helpers within the many thousands of households in Hong Kong. Caucasians are the third largest minority group, at 0.5 per cent of the population.

1.1 History

Hong Kong came under direct British rule in 1842, with the signing of the Treaty of Nanking. The name Hong Kong (香港) is not attested in written sources until that date. Prior to that, in the mid-1700s, there had been an imperial decree restricting commercial activity with the rest of the world to Guangzhou (Canton). Guangzhou had subsequently become a centre for the tea trade (Bolton 2003), which drew trading ships from Britain and other countries to this region of China. It was not until the events of the Opium Wars that Britain was able to take control of Hong Kong Island in 1841, and subsequently the Kowloon Peninsula in 1860. Britain was granted a 99-year lease of the New Territories, including Lantau Island, in 1898. In 1984, the British and the Chinese governments signed a treaty known as the Sino-British Joint Declaration, which provided for the return of Hong Kong to Chinese rule at the end of the lease. At midnight on 30 June 1997, that lease came to an end, and administrative control of the whole of the region was returned to the PRC. That event has come to be known as the Handover. It was stipulated in the Joint Declaration that the PRC would govern Hong Kong as a Special Administrative Region, and undertake to retain its laws and a high degree of autonomy for at least fifty years after the Handover; this is reflected in the term 'one country, two systems'. Hong Kong, which grew to be a major centre for banking and commerce in the South East Asia region under British rule, has continued to thrive, and English has continued to be used. In Chapter 6, there is further discussion of the history of Hong Kong from a linguistic perspective, particularly with reference to English.

1.2 Languages

The language situation can be described as 'trilingual and biliterate'. 'Trilingual' refers to Hong Kong's three official spoken languages: Cantonese, English and Putonghua (spoken Mandarin Chinese), while 'biliterate' refers to the two written languages used by the average Hongkonger: written Standard Chinese and English.

According to the statistics of the official government website (available at www.gov.hk/en/about/abouthk/facts.htm), Cantonese speakers form the majority of the population. The figures of the percentage of speakers of various mother-tongue languages within the Hong Kong population, as at April 2009, are as follows: Cantonese speakers 88.7 per cent; speakers of other Chinese dialects 5.8 per cent; English speakers

3.1 per cent; Putonghua speakers 1.1 per cent; speakers of other languages 1.3 per cent.

While both Chinese and English are the official languages of Hong Kong, for historical reasons English is the predominant language of the government, the legal system, and the professional and business sectors. All official signs are written in both English and traditional Chinese characters. The average Hongkonger is mostly bilingual; they are able to communicate in Cantonese and simple English. After the return of sovereignty of Hong Kong to China, the official language of China, Putonghua, has gained more prominence in the local language landscape. More and more are becoming trilingual since 1997, due to the fact that Putonghua has been introduced into the curriculum in the education system and that increasing numbers of tourists visiting Hong Kong are from mainland China. Most taxi drivers and salespersons nowadays are able to communicate in English and Putonghua, with varying levels of proficiency, in addition to Cantonese. This variation in proficiency fuels the debate about whether Hong Kong English is a variety in its own right, or a learner interlanguage; we discuss this issue in Chapter 6, where we look at the context, status and current state of development of Hong Kong English.

The language situation in education differs from other official areas of English use. Before the Handover in 1997, the vast majority of secondary schools used English as the medium of instruction. Immediately after the Handover, however, that policy changed, as the government preferred that schools use the mother tongue (that is, Cantonese), except in English lessons. Li (1999) observes that there was conflict between the government's policy of 'mother-tongue education' and parents' preference for English. This is another area we take up for further discussion in Chapter 6.

Outside the realm of education, English is an important lingua franca for Hong Kong. This is not intranational usage, as in Singapore or India, for example, but as a means of communication with the outside world, in the fields of banking and finance, business, and the tourism and hospitality industry. Multinational corporations are known to choose Hong Kong as the site for their Asia-Pacific headquarters. Business in these corporations is largely conducted in English (Hyland 1997: 193); one survey reports that English is used in over 66 per cent of communication in the workplace (Blomfield and Pierson 1987, cited in Hyland 1997: 193), although it may be assumed that much of this is written communication. Those wishing to do business with China consider Hong Kong to be a desirable location, in that it is well known as a successful centre for international finance and trade, and English has clearly been

Table 1.1 Some examples of English loanwords in Cantonese (Bauer and Wong 2008)

English source	Loanword in Cantonese
bus	巴士baa1 si2
chance	餐屍caan1 si2
taxi	的士dik1 si2
store	士多si6 do1
OK	OK ou1 kei1
X-ray	X 光 ik1 si4 gwong1

a factor in this success (Hyland 1997: 193). Given this, it is understandable that English should be perceived as a socially prestigious language, associated with increased income and a high level of education (Cheng and Zi 1987).

Language contact has naturally led to linguistic borrowing. In an international city like Hong Kong, the blending of Chinese, English and other Asian cultures has resulted in numerous loanwords widely used among local Hong Kong people. Although English and Cantonese are typologically quite distinct languages, this has not impeded the mutual borrowing of lexical items between the two. Wong et al. (2009: 252) indicate that contact between English and Cantonese speakers began as early as 'the late 17th century when British traders came to Canton to buy Chinese tea and porcelain and has continued to the present'. The first English–Cantonese, Cantonese–English dictionary, *A Vocabulary of the Canton Dialect*, authored by Robert Morrison and published in 1828, gives evidence of English loanwords in Cantonese at the time of publication. Starting in the 1960s, loanwords in Hong Kong Cantonese have attracted the attention of such linguists as Cowles (1965), Cheung (1972), Kiu (1977), Chan and Kwok (1982, 1985) and Bauer and Benedict (1997). Bauer and Wong (2008) have compiled a set of more than 700 entries of English loanwords in Hong Kong Cantonese. Table 1.1 gives some examples.[3]

At the same time, some Cantonese lexical items have entered the English language (Chan and Kwok 1985); Table 1.2 gives some examples of these.

1.3 Cultural factors

Although Hong Kong is a region where Chinese and westerners live quite peacefully together, it is culturally still very Chinese. For one thing, the majority of the population of Hong Kong is ethnic Chinese.

Table 1.2 Some examples of Cantonese loanwords in English (Chan and Kwok 1985)

Cantonese source	Loanword in English	Gloss
點心 dim2 sam1	dim sum	tidbits eaten at a Cantonese restaurant
雲吞 wan4 tan1	wonton	Cantonese dumplings
白菜 baak6 coi3	bok choy	Chinese cabbage
茄汁 ke2 zap1	ketchup	tomato sauce
長衫 coeng4 saam1	cheongsam	a long garment worn by Chinese women
鬼佬 gwai2 lou2	gweilo	'ghost man', referring to western men
三板 saam1 baan2	sampan	Chinese small boat

In addition, Hong Kong's relationship with mainland China has never been severed in spite of the period of British colonial rule and China's closed-door policy, which lasted from the establishment of the PRC in 1949 until the early 1980s. However, when compared to other Chinese cities, Hong Kong is the most cosmopolitan of all. This is why Hong Kong is unique.

Most Hong Kong people still uphold traditional Chinese values such as filial piety, family harmony, a patriarchal society, and the importance of their roots in mainland China. However, the same Hong Kong people are influenced by western liberal ideas and place the utmost importance on individuality. The modern nuclear family unit is in stark contrast to the traditional Chinese extended family structure, but almost all of Hong Kong's families have followed the modern trend of forming such nuclear families.

The lifestyles of Hong Kong people also reflect the blending of 'east' and 'west'. While Chinese cuisine is the still the default choice for most families when it comes to food, some families, especially those in the middle class, very often will opt for western meals. The great variety of choice of restaurants in the town centres reflects the mix of eastern and western cultures in Hong Kong. Festivals in Hong Kong are another example of how Chinese and western cultures have influenced the lifestyles of Hong Kong people. Both the western New Year and the Chinese New Year are celebrated. Traditional Chinese festivals such as the Dragon Boat Festival, Mid-Autumn Festival, Ching Ming and Chung Yeung are celebrated alongside major western festivals such as Christmas and Easter. One typical example which illustrates the mix of the two cultures in Hong Kong can be found in the numbering of floors in buildings. Since the number 4 in Cantonese sounds similar to the word referring to death, the fourth floor is sometimes not found in some buildings. By the same token, the thirteenth floor can also be found missing from these buildings, because the number 13 is considered to bring bad luck.

Hong Kong people have always faced an identity crisis, for both political and historical reasons. As ethnic Chinese ruled by British colonial governors for almost a century, it would have been natural for Hongkongers to rejoice when Hong Kong's sovereignty was returned to China. However, under British rule, Hong Kong became a capitalist society while China remained a communist system, and for this reason most Hongkongers did not feel they would readily identify themselves as national 'Chinese'. Also, the political turmoil that China has undergone under communist rule led most Hongkongers to believe that they would want to stay as far away from the government of the PRC as possible. Hence, Hong Kong witnessed an exodus of citizens during the late 1980s and early 1990s in the face of reunification with China.

After the Handover, especially with the opening up of China and the rise of China to supremacy on the international political stage, more and more Hongkongers have become willing to define themselves as 'Chinese'. In spite of this, a lot of Hong Kong citizens still insist their nationality is 'Hong Kong' – neither British nor Chinese.

1.4 Variation in Hong Kong English

Hong Kong English is an emergent variety and, as such, speakers are likely to vary greatly in their ability to use the language. This is not unusual in varieties of English. In British English, for example, the term 'Estuary English' (Rosewarne 1984, 1994a, 1994b; see also Przedlacka 2002) is often thought to refer to a defined group of speakers, but is in fact an umbrella term for a set of what are largely pronunciation features, such as l-vocalisation and t-glottaling, which appear in the speech of British speakers from Southend in Essex to Ramsgate in Kent, Swindon in Wiltshire and beyond; these speakers do not all adopt every feature of Estuary English. Closer to home, Deterding (2007: 6) refers to the 'substantial variation in the English of Singapore', pointing out that features like age, ethnic background and level of education will play a part. Ethnic background is much less of a concern in Hong Kong English, but age and education level may well result in differences.

The data we use here to exemplify phonological, grammatical and discourse features were taken from a group of five Hong Kong English speakers recorded in the UK. At first, we were concerned that these speakers would have been influenced too much by their British environment, but in the data we collected all the features we expected to find were present, even in the speech of the subject who had been in the UK for eighteen months. K. K. Luke (personal communication) observed that the Hong Kong English of adults abroad does not seem to be very much affected by their environment; the first author's experience of Hongkongers in the UK leads us to concur.

1.5 Data from our speakers

The subjects whose spoken data we use in this book to exemplify the features of Hong Kong English were all students in their twenties studying in the UK at either the University of Reading or the University of Oxford. The interviewer is European, but not a native speaker of English. We originally collected data from eleven speakers, all of whom signed consent forms for their data to be used for research purposes, and five of whom gave permission for their data to be used in this book. The five had been in the UK for varying amounts of time, from two weeks to eighteen months. Subjects were asked to recount a happy event from some point in their lives, often childhood, and to perform a map task[+] activity, a co-operative task in which they were required to guide the interviewer from a starting point to the meeting point on a map which they both held, but on which only the subjects had the route. There were some differences in detail in the maps; for example, both had a rope bridge in the same location, but only one had crocodiles under the bridge. The data were originally collected in order to examine the acoustic features of intonation in Hong Kong English in a study supported by the University of Reading's Research Endowment Trust Fund; at the time of writing, this research is yet to be carried out in any detail. The subjects' profiles are given in Table 1.3.

Data were collected using a Sony Minidisk recorder with a lapel microphone fixed close to the subject's mouth, but not directly in front of it. This means that the subjects are loud and clear on the whole, but that the interviewer is usually much fainter. Recordings were made in a sound-treated room at the Universities of Reading and Oxford, and then transferred on to computer and saved in wave format. We accept that the method of recording has meant that the data were not collected in a naturalistic setting, but feel that the compromise was justified in terms of the quality of the data which resulted; speech data of a certain quality are required in order to do acoustic measurement of the signal, which was the original purpose for data collection. Other collections of Hong Kong English speech data exist, such as the Hong Kong Corpus of Spoken English (see Cheng et al. 2008), but have not been recorded in conditions which make the speech suitable for acoustic analysis.

Table 1.3 Details of the Hong Kong English speakers whose data are used in this book

Subject	Gender	Age	Length of time in the UK	Other time spent outside Hong Kong	English-language qualifications
1	Male	20	18 months	None	TOEFL[a] 230/300
5	Female	24	7 months	None	IELTS[b] 8; HKCEE[c] C; HKUE[d] D
8	Female	20	2 weeks	Short visits to Canada	IELTS 7.5; HKCEE A
9	Male	27	6 months	None	IELTS 7.5; HKCEE C; HKUE C
10	Female	27	6 months	None	IELTS 8; HKCEE C

[a] Test of English as a Foreign Language.
[b] International English Language Testing System.
[c] Hong Kong Certificate of Education Examination (similar to GCSE in the UK).
[d] Hong Kong Advanced Level Use of English (similar to A-level in the UK).

Readers who are interested in the speech data used for the book are invited to visit www.reading.ac.uk/epu/HKE to download the files. Excerpts are given in the text with a reference tag following to show which file is being used, and the time in minutes and seconds at which the excerpt occurs. 'MT' refers to map task files and 'HE' refers to happy event files. For example, the reference {01-MT:01:20} indicates Speaker 1's map task file starting at 1 minute and 20 seconds. The full orthographic transcripts are included in Chapter 8.

1.6 Other data used

In Chapter 5, examples of Cantonese–English code-switching are drawn from previous literature and more recent data from television and radio, and in these examples the source is acknowledged.

1.7 Outline of the book

This volume on Hong Kong English proceeds from here with Chapter 2 on phonetics and phonology, Chapter 3 on morphology and syntax, and Chapter 4 on discourse features. In each case, examples are extracted from our Hong Kong English speakers' data, but there is also reference to other works. Chapter 5 is on code-switching; as one would expect from conversation with a non-Cantonese speaker, this does not occur very often in our speech data, and so other sources are also referred to here. Chapter 6 discusses the history of English in Hong Kong, and assesses sociolinguistic aspects, as well as the arguments for and against the existence of a variety called Hong Kong English. Chapter 7 is an annotated bibliography of works on the variety, and finally Chapter 8 contains the transcripts of the data collected from Speakers 1, 5, 8, 9 and 10.

Notes

1. The description cited is taken from the official internet website of the Hong Kong Special Administrative Region, accessed on 1 April 2009: http://www.gov.hk/en/about/abouthk/facts.htm. We consider the official government website of Hong Kong to be a reliable source of information.

2. An interactive map of Hong Kong and the region can be viewed on the website of the Hong Kong Tourism Board: http://www.discover-hongkong.com/eng/trip-planner/hongkong-maps.html.

3. The transcription of Cantonese in this book follows the Cantonese Romanisation Scheme (Jyut6 Ping3/粵拼) devised by the Linguistic Society of Hong Kong (1997). The number (from 1 to 6) at the end of a syllable indicates different tones in Cantonese. See http://www.lshk.org/cantonese.php for details.

4. The map task activity we used is part of a collection of such tasks devised by the Human Communication Research Centre at the University of Edinburgh. See http://www.hcrc.ed.ac.uk/maptask/ for more information.

2 Phonetics and phonology

Hong Kong English is an emergent new variety and, as such, its status as either a legitimate variety or learner interlanguage is under dispute. Some writers prefer to discuss phonological aspects of Hong Kong English in terms of error when compared to varieties such as British or American English (see, for example, Stibbard 2004; Chan 2006; Chan and Li 2000). This chapter – and, indeed, this book – does not take this view, preferring to describe and evaluate Hong Kong English pronunciation on its own terms, and in terms of difference from other accents rather than deficiency. However, it should be recognised that, as it is an emergent new variety, features of Hong Kong English such as phonology are not always stable, and that there is wide variation amongst speakers in both intelligibility and similarity to other accents and varieties. It is therefore necessary to talk in terms of tendencies in phonology, rather than to assume all speakers share the same characteristics.

The pronunciation of English in Hong Kong varies along a continuum from native-like British English Received Pronunciation (RP) and/or General American accent features to virtual unintelligibility outside of the Hong Kong environment. What may be thought of as the typical Hong Kong English accent (see, for example, Deterding et al. 2008; Hung 2000; Peng and Setter 2000), spoken by educated individuals who have not spent much, if any, time outside of Hong Kong, is clearly influenced by features of Cantonese phonology. For example, Hong Kong English speakers often avoid consonant clusters, not generally found in Cantonese, and in particular clusters in word-final position, which can affect morphology in terms of past tense and plural, third person or possessive markers (see Chapter 3). Hong Kong English vowels are of interest as Cantonese, like English, is a vowel-rich language, but phoneme categories are not generally similar in English and Cantonese, and this can lead to differences in vowel realisation in comparison with, for example, RP. Concerning suprasegmental features, Hong Kong English word and sentence stress patterns, speech rhythm and intonation all have characteristics which are identifiable in speakers of the variety.

In this chapter, we will focus on areas of pronunciation which are typical among Hong Kong English speakers, while recognising that there is considerable variation amongst speakers. We will start by looking at consonants before going on to consider vowels. We will end with a look at some of the suprasegmental aspects of the variety. Examples will be extracted from the recordings of our Hong Kong English speakers.

2.1 The consonantal inventory

There has been more than one attempt to list the consonants and vowels of Hong Kong English (for example, Deterding et al. 2008; Hung 2000; Chan and Li 2000; Bolton and Kwok 1990), and on the whole there is agreement amongst them. From these studies, it is possible to give the phonemic consonantal inventory in Table 2.1 as that of a typical Hong Kong English speaker, with voiced variants appearing on the right of each cell and voiceless ones on the left.

We have listed /w/ under 'bilabial' and 'velar' here; it is in fact labial-velar. The consonants given in parentheses in this table, all voiced frica-tives, are considered to be 'marginal'; these are discussed in more detail in the section which follows.

2.2 Voicing contrasts and glottal stops

Voicing of consonants is one area in which Hong Kong English has very distinctive patterns. We can observe three main tendencies: the main-tenance of voicing contrast in initial plosives and affricates, the loss of voicing contrast in final plosives and affricates, and the loss of voicing contrasts in fricatives wherever they occur.

Where plosive and affricate consonants are concerned, in syllable-initial position, Hong Kong English clearly has a voicing contrast. This contrast is not unlike that of other varieties such as RP and General American, in that the chief difference between voiceless and voiced phonemes is the aspiration of voiceless phonemes. Hung (2000: 347) notes that the voiced consonants /b/, /d/, /g/ and /dʒ/ 'are not truly voiced' but, as is the convention with other varieties with similar phonological patterns, prefers to use the terms 'voiceless' and 'voiced' rather than 'aspirated' and 'unaspirated'. He also notes that these con-sonants contrast in word-medial position through the maintenance of aspiration in voiceless sounds (Hung 2000: 347). Cantonese, the first language of Hong Kong English speakers, has quite strongly aspirated

Table 2.1 A consonantal phoneme inventory for Hong Kong English

	Bilabial	Labiodental	Dental	Alveolar	Postalveolar	Palatal	Velar	Glottal
Plosive	p b			t d			k g	
Nasal	m			n			ŋ	
Fricative		f (v)	θ (ð)	s (z)	ʃ (ʒ)			h
Affricate				tʃ dʒ				
Median approximant	w			r		j	w	
Lateral approximant				l				

plosives; Lisker and Abramson (1964, cited in Cho and Ladefoged 1999) demonstrate that the distinction in Cantonese between aspirated and unaspirated plosive consonants is a voice onset time (VOT) of 79–98 ms (milliseconds) for the former and 9–34 ms for the latter, and that this is significantly higher than in varieties of English such as RP and General American; for comparison, Cruttenden (2008: 160) gives the VOT of voiceless (aspirated) plosives in RP as 40–75ms, and explains that in RP voiced plosives the VOT is much smaller and can be negative.

In syllable-final position, however, the voicing contrast tends to disappear in plosives, and is variable concerning affricates. Hung (2000) suggests that the main difference is in the aspirated release of voiceless stops and the inaudible release of voiced stops, but gives no examples himself, and this is not attested in other studies. Chan and Li (2000: 78) claim that speakers of Hong Kong English cannot 'actualise the systematic contrast between voiced and voiceless final plosives', in that both voiced and voiceless variants are unreleased. In Cantonese, there is no voicing contrast in final plosive consonants; the three final stop consonants are /p/, /t/ and /k/, which are produced with strong glottal reinforcement and are not released (see Cheung 1986). In Hong Kong English, this pattern is often imposed on final plosive consonants, and is a prevalent feature of the variety. In combination with clipping of the preceding vowel in all environments, this leads to the perceived lack of contrast. An example of strong glottal reinforcement of /p/ can be heard in Speaker 1's production of *rope bridge* in extract (1) and Speaker 9's production of *sport* in extract (2), which sounds very much like *spot*:

(1) actually you should go through the rope bridge [ɹoʊʔp̚brɪdʒ]

{01-MT:06:27}

(2) and like sport [spɔʔt] game

{09-HE:07:23}

The /dʒ/ in *rope bridge*, however, is not produced as the voiceless variant by Speaker 1. In the following example from Speaker 5, the /d/ of *word* is replaced with a glottal stop in extract (3), and in Speaker 10's production of *weekend* the /k/ is realised as a glottal stop, even though the following sound is a vowel (4):

(3) so that the first word [wɜʔ] *mat6* is similar

{05-HE:09:02}

(4) some places with my father at weekend [wiʔɛn]

{10-HE:00:05}

This strong glottal reinforcement or replacement of final plosive consonants is a very obvious characteristic of Hong Kong English speech,
and together with other features, such as speech rhythm, can result in
the variety sounding staccato or 'choppy' in a similar way to Singapore
English (see Brown 1988; Deterding 2007).

Table 2.1 gives voiced fricative consonants in parentheses to indicate
that they are marginal, as often they are not produced as such by Hong
Kong English speakers. These consonants may, however, be realised in
a variety of ways, not just as their voiceless counterparts. Hung (2000)
demonstrates quite clearly that there is no contrast between voiced
and voiceless fricatives in Hong Kong English, and comments that the
patterns are different from other varieties in the region. Here are some
examples of the production of the fricatives /ʒ/ in *usually* and /z/ in
cousins by Speaker 1 and Speaker 5:

(5) my dad usually [juʃəli] drive his car and pick us up

{01-HE:00:17}

(6) I have a brother and many cousins [kʌsəns] of similar ages

{05-HE:00:10}

Hung (2000) gives evidence for one alveolar fricative, /s/, and one
palato-alveolar fricative /ʃ/ (although we certainly find voiced alveolar
fricatives in our data; see extracts (10) and (20) below). In words where a
back rounded vowel follows /s/, however, the sound may be realised as
[ʃ], in which case there is a loss of contrast between the two phonemes;
Chan and Li (2000: 79) give the example *soup*, which may be produced
[ʃup]. In our recordings, Speaker 10 does something similar with the
word *zoo*, where she produces a voiceless palato-alveolar fricative rather
than a voiced alveolar one in extract (7):

(7) yeah quite like a zoo [ʃu]

{10-HE:02:56}

Figure 2.1 shows a spectrographic display of *like a zoo* from extract (7),
specifically the section where Speaker 10 produces the [s]. It is clear that
the consonant is not voiced: the voicing for the preceding and following
vowels is indicated by the dark horizontal bands, known as formants,
which appear at a low level on either side of the consonant. We can
see that the sound in the section indicated is a fricative from the dark,
'messy' pattern at the top of the section, indicating air turbulence which
is irregular or aperiodic in frequency, as opposed to the more regular

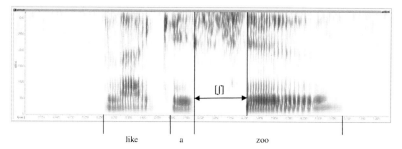

like   a   zoo

Figure 2.1 Spectrographic display of *like a zoo* with the [ʃ] in *zoo* indicated, as produced by Speaker 10

or periodic pattern shown by the vertical striations in the neighbouring voiced sounds.

Hung (2000) demonstrates that the voiced labiodental fricative /v/ is not produced as such in Hong Kong English, but that it is realised either as [w] or [f]. The data he initially presents suggest that [w] occurs at the beginning of a stressed syllable and [f] at the beginning of an unstressed syllable, but in fact further data show that morphemically similar pairs such as *televise* and *television* both contain [w]. Our data suggest that the production of [v]/[w]/[f] could be lexically motivated, and that individual variation is quite high. There are clear examples of substitution of [f] and [w] for /v/ in both stressed and unstressed positions in Speaker 9's production of *arrive, very* and *environment* in extract (8), and in Speaker 1's production of *view point* in extract (9):

(8) while we arrive [ə'raɪf] we can see a very ['wɛri] beautiful environment [ɛn'fɐʊmɛnʔ]

{09-HE:01:06}

(9) springboks should be . . . on the highest viewpoint [fiu'pɔɪnt] . . . left

{01-MT:01:41}

2.3 Dental fricatives

Production issues with dental fricatives in varieties of English, such as Wells' (1982) account of TH-fronting in Cockney and TH-stopping in Cockney and Irish English, are well attested. Jenkins (2000), who studied intelligibility in non-native-speaker-English interactions, does not include /θ/ and /ð/ in her Lingua Franca Core, which indicates that they are in fact neither widespread in varieties of English around the world nor essential for being understood. Looking at patterns of dental fricative usage in Hong Kong English, we can see that speakers vary in their use of these sounds (see Deterding et al. 2008), and often substitute other consonants. Where these substitutions take place, the usual production of /θ/ is [f] (fronting), and of /ð/ it is [d] (stopping). We can find various examples of this throughout the data, particularly in the map task material, where there is a lot of reference to *north* and *south*; here are some examples from Speakers 1 and 9:

(10) so there's [dɛəz] actually a path [pɑf] between those [ðoʊz] two
{01-MT:01:53}

(11) or you should go south [saʊf] I should say
{01-MT:04:00}

(12) you should turn left half way through [fru]
{01-MT:06:19}

(13) now go south [saʊf]
{09-MT:00:17}

(14) pass through [fru] it and then go north [nɔf]
{09-MT:01:16}

Stopping of the voiceless sound is not unheard of, however, and there is an example of this from Speaker 5:

(15) and then I think [tɪŋ] um he said
{05-HE:08:06}

There is also a final cluster simplification in the production of *think* in this example, which brings us neatly on to the next topic.

2.4 Final consonant cluster simplification

Like many other varieties of English spoken in the region (see, for example, Deterding 2007 on Singapore English), in Hong Kong English, consonant clusters at the ends of words are often simplified, and it is uncommon for syllables to end with clusters of more than two consonants; Setter (2008a) found none. Peng and Setter (2000) demonstrated that the process was highly systematic, in that /t/ and /d/ were often omitted in syllable-final consonant clusters in particular environments. This is not an unusual phenomenon in varieties of English, and indeed cluster simplification is a common process in RP, but there are some differences between the circumstances under which elision of /t/ and /d/ take place in Hong Kong English and in RP. For example, unlike in RP, elision may take place before a vowel in Hong Kong English, or before a pause, as shown in the following examples from Speaker 9:

(16) er then you go east [is] . . . until you see a springboks

{09-MT:00:26}

(17) so you keep going east [is] . . . um

{09-MT:00:53}

It can also take place following a vowel but preceding a consonant; Peng and Setter (2000) give *boats* pronounced [bəʊs] as one example. Speaker 5 consistently produces *it's* with an elided /t/ in examples such as those which follow:

(18) and actually it's [ɪs] very nice it's [ɪs] like a house with rooms it's [ɪs] got partitions

{05-HE:02:09}

(19) no it's [ɪs] not it's [ɪs] probably something for I think um some toys

{05-HE:02:21}

This is unlike the pattern in RP, in which /t/ and /d/ are usually only elided when one of them is the middle consonant in a group of three, in which the first consonant agrees with the /t/ or /d/ in voicing, and where the first and second consonants must be word-final (Cruttenden 2008: 303–4). Elision of /t/, for example, usually takes place in *tests* in RP, but not in *eats*, where the consonant is preceded by a vowel.

In one instance in the data, there is a misunderstanding between Speaker 10 and the Interviewer owing to a missing /d/:

(20) 10: and we play some er . . . small scale rides [raɪz] there for children rides

Int: small scale rise

10: the rides the rides [raɪdz] yeah for children's

{10-HE:00:44}

Deterding et al. (2008) show in their data that /t/ is deleted in 47.2 per cent of instances where it is the final consonant in a cluster, and /d/

is deleted 62.5 per cent of the time. However, in Deterding et al.'s Hong Kong English data, in comparison with Singapore English, a relatively high number of final /t/ and /d/ consonants in clusters are retained. There is also evidence for the omission of /k/, which is not commonly elided in varieties such as British English. There is an example of /k/ elision in the word *think*, realised as [tɪŋ], in (15) above.

Speaker 9 regularly elides /p/ at the end of *camp* in the phrase *wild camp*. This, together with the speaker's vocalised /l/ (see section 2.5 below), leads to the Interviewer requesting clarification:

(21) 09: and the church organise a a wild camp [waɪo kɛm] activities ...
           so um
      Int: wild camp [waɪld kæmp] or isn't it
      09: wild wild camp [waɪo? waɪo kɛm]

{09-HE:00:20}

Hong Kong English speakers may also avoid final consonant clusters by inserting epenthetic vowels, particularly where an *-ed* ending results in a cluster. This is demonstrated by Speaker 9 in his production of the word *equipped* in the following example, where he inserts a vowel between the last two consonants:

(22) they are more well equipped [ikwɪpɪ?]

{09-HE:03:08}

In opposition to the phenomenon of final consonant cluster reduction is that of consonant addition. Setter and Deterding (2003) report on the addition of extra final consonants [s], [t] and [k] to the ends of words in Singapore and Hong Kong English. There is no clear reason why this might be so; one possible suggestion is hypercorrection, in that the speakers know they often simplify clusters and so are attempting to compensate, but the evidence is inconclusive. Some examples of extra final consonants in the data of Speakers 10 and 9 are given in extracts (23) and (24). While the [s] at the end of *scales* could be an example of hypercorrection (in that the grammatical subject is plural), the [d] at the end of *way* cannot.

(23) so they are in a very small scales

{10-HE:00:55}

(24) at the mid-way [weɪd] of banana tree and rock fill

{09-MT:03:08}

2.5 /l/-vocalisation

A very obvious feature of Hong Kong English is /l/-vocalisation when /l/ is at the end of the syllable. /l/-vocalisation is almost certain to occur, even when a syllable is followed by a vowel. We can see examples of /l/-vocalisation in Speaker 1's production of *able* and *field*, and Speakers 5 and 9's production of *until* (vocalised /l/ is shown using the symbol [o]):

(25) and you should be able [eɪbo] to see a safari truck

{01-MT:02:10}

(26) and then you should be able [eɪbo] to see a field [fiod] station

{01-MT:02:45}

(27) now go south until [ʌntio] you pass the diamond mine

{09-MT:00:16}

(28) I think until [ʌntio] I got to primary school

{05-HE:06:23}

Owing to this phenomenon, Setter (2008a) found no instances of final clusters where /l/ precedes another consonant, and Wong and Setter (2002) found only three examples of /l/ being produced in a final cluster out of forty-six possible instances. Speaker 5 gives an example of an instance in which such a cluster might occur were /l/ not vocalised:

(29) I got a quite interesting childhood [tʃaɪodhud]

{05-HE:00:00}

2.6 The /n/–/l/ merger

In some cases, /l/ is produced as [n] by speakers of Hong Kong English, and /n/ is produced as [l]. This may be owing to language transfer from the well-documented /n/–/l/ merger that is taking place in Cantonese, first identified by Chao (1947), confirmed by Bauer (1982), and more recently reported as a widespread 'unconditioned merging' amongst young speakers of Hong Kong Cantonese by Zee (1996) and Bauer and Benedict (1997). Zee (1996: 192) notes that there are only 'isolated cases where the speakers have retained [n]', whilst Bauer and Benedict (1997: 24) observe that 'words which are pronounced in standard Cantonese with *n*- regularly take *l*- in the speech of many speakers in Hong Kong'.

They go on to say that this merger does not seem to have impacted negatively on communication. However, the alternations of syllable-initial /n/ and /l/ in the English produced by some of the young Cantonese speakers in Hong Kong do sometimes impede communication, as we will see in extract (30) below.

The phenomenon is by no means common to all speakers of Hong Kong English, and not entirely predictable by rule when it does occur. Wong and Setter (2002) studied /n/–/l/ merging in Hong Kong English speakers and found that, in over 900 tokens produced in conversation, the phenomenon occurred in only 87 instances, which is less than 9 per cent. Where there were instances of merging, it was more often the case that /n/ was produced as [l] rather than the reverse. Wong and Setter (2002) also observed that the pattern of substitution was not entirely random, in that merging tended to take place at the beginning of a stressed syllable, although this was a tendency rather than a rule. Also, in multisyllabic words or phrases such as *Polytechnic University*, speakers tended to select either [n] or [l] and stick with it throughout, yielding either [pɔli'tɛʔlɪk juli'wɜsiti] or [pɔni'tɛʔnɪk juni'wɜsiti]; this process is sometimes referred to as 'consonant harmony'.

In our data, Speaker 9's production of *snake* uses [l] in extract (30), and in the phrase *not alone* he demonstrates consonant harmony in his selection of [n] in extract (31):

(30) or even snake [slɛʔk]

{09-HE:04:41}

(31) yes we are not alone [nɔʔ ə'noʊn]

{09-HE:06:30}

Speaker 9 is able to produce *snake* with [n], however, as he does so when this word is queried by the interviewer, but interestingly the interviewer has already produced the phrase *not alone* immediately before Speaker 9's turn, and Speaker 9 does not copy him; whether there is a need to accommodate to the listener in order to communicate information clearly may therefore play a role in a speaker's ability to disambiguate /n/ and /l/.

Speaker 10 demonstrates consonant harmony when she produces the phrase *no longer* with [n]:

(32) so it's no longer [noʊ nɔŋgə] here

{10-HE:00:29}

2.7 Diphthongs followed by consonants

In the example above from Speaker 9 (30), we see him produce *snake* as [slɛʔk]. Where a diphthong is followed by a consonant at the end of a word in Hong Kong English, one of three things may happen: the diphthong is preserved and the consonant disappears; the consonant is produced but the diphthong is realised as a monophthong; both the diphthong and the consonant are produced. Here are some examples of the first two phenomena:

(33) we you know decorate [dɛkərɛt] our house

{01-HE:02:19}

(34) 'cause I think at the beginning it was like that size [saɪ]

{05-HE:04:26}

(35) and then I fell off to the other side [saɪ] into the field

{05-HE:05:31}

(36) so we are at the starting point [pɔnt] and do you see a diamond mine [maɪ]

{09-MT:00:00}

In examples (34) and (35) above from Speaker 5, there is a loss of contrast between the words *size* and *side* owing to the loss of the final consonant, although the meaning is recoverable from the context. In the case of a following nasal, the vowel may be quite strongly nasalised, and that can be heard in Speaker 9's production of *mine* in example (36).

A possible account for the issues involved in articulating a diphthong followed by a consonant in Hong Kong English is that in Cantonese, while diphthongs and final consonants are present, it is not possible to have both in one syllable, and this pattern is transferred to the production of English when such sequences arise. From a phonological perspective, the glide (that is, the second) element of a diphthong fulfils the position of a final consonant in Cantonese, in which CVC is the maximum syllable. (C stands for *consonant* and V for *vowel*.) See Cheung (1986: 87) and Matthews and Yip (1994: 19) for more detail.

2.8 Initial consonant cluster simplification

Final clusters are not the only sequences to undergo simplification; initial clusters may also be simplified by Hong Kong English speakers. In particular, an approximant consonant following an initial labial obstruent may in some instances be deleted. However, this is particularly inconsistent in the data. Here are some examples where simplification occurs:

(37) I think until I got to primary [paɪmri] school

{05-HE:06:23}

(38) and we play [peɪ] some er . . . small scale rides there

{10-HE:00:44}

(39) she took me to many places [peɪsɛz]

{08-HE:00:57}

(40) took a flight [faɪt] back

{08-HE:01:58}

Speaker 9, however, adds an /r/ in the word *fee*, which could be a slip of the tongue given the context, or owing to the neighbouring r-cluster in *entrance*:

(41) so the entrance fee [friː] and the food are relatively cheap

{09-HE:07:36}

In words where a palatal glide comes after a consonant, as in *few* in the next example, the glide element may be produced as a vowel.

(42) and then I remember that . . . um my cousin they actually took a few [fiu] back home

{05-HE:03:08}

2.9 *You* pronounced [tʃu]

Some Hong Kong English speakers pronounce the word *you* with a [tʃ] onset. Speaker 5 does this mostly in the phrase *you know*, but not exclusively. Here are some examples of her production of *you* with the [tʃ] onset.

(43) so um they . . . you [tʃu] wouldn't believe their life

{05-HE:07:08}

(44) cause I felt very embarrassed of you [tʃu] know not um knowing something that they said

{05-HE:09:41}

SUPRASEGMENTAL TONE T		
ONSET	RIME or FINAL	
INITIAL Initial Consonant C_i	NUCLEUS	CODA
	Nuclear Vowel V or Syllabic Consonant C_{syl}	Final Consonant C_f

Figure 2.2 Structural components of the Cantonese syllable (Bauer and Benedict 1997: 314)

The possibility that Speaker 5 is producing *you know* as *d'you know* in these extracts could be the explanation in extract (44), but not in extract (43); there is also no reason for the pronoun to be preceded by another consonant in extract (43), as it follows a pause.

2.10 Influences from Cantonese on consonants in Hong Kong English

It is without a doubt that there is some influence from the phonology of Cantonese on the production of consonants in Hong Kong English. Cantonese differs from English not only in terms of individual segments, but also in syllable structure.

Cheung (1986: 29) views the syllable as the 'primary phonological isolate' in Cantonese. Bauer and Benedict (1997) give the chart shown in Figure 2.2, which includes syllabic consonants, and gives tone T as a separate suprasegmental element. As before, C stands for *consonant* and V for *vowel* in this chart; note that C_f may be a glide as well as an occlusive consonant such as a nasal or plosive.

In initial position in Cantonese syllables, the consonants shown in Table 2.2 are possible. As mentioned above, aspiration is a major factor in Cantonese initial plosive consonants.

In particular, there is palatalisation of affricates preceding the close, front and rounded Cantonese vowel [y], so for example /ts/ is realised as [tʃ] in words such as *zyu6[1]* (*live*) (Matthews and Yip 1994: 14). As seen in section 2.2 extract (7), this can have an effect on the pronunciation of similar sequences in Hong Kong English.

From this description, it can be deduced that Cantonese does not allow consonant cluster combinations in initial position, unlike English, which may have up to three consonants initially (see, for example, Roach 2009: 56–8). Syllable-finally, only the following occlusive consonants are

Table 2.2 A consonantal phoneme inventory for Cantonese (adapted from Bauer and Benedict 1997: 17)

	Unaspirated	Aspirated	Fricative	Nasal	Approximant	Lateral
Labial	p	ph	f	m		
Dental/alveolar	t	th	s	n		l
Velar/glottal	k	kh	h	ŋ		
Labial-velar	kŵ	kĥw			w	
Affricate	ts	tsh				
Palatal					j	

allowed: /p/, /t/, /k/, /m/, /n/ and /ŋ/ (Cheung 1986; see also Walton 1983: 33; Matthews and Yip 1994: 15), and it is possible to see that they are in pairs of the same place of articulation, bilabial /p/ and /m/, alveolar /t/ and /n/, and velar /k/ and /ŋ/. Those syllables ending in a syllable-final plosive consonant are considerably shorter than others, and this has an effect on the rhythm of Hong Kong English (see section 2.16 below).

Only one consonant is permitted at the end of a syllable in Cantonese, in contrast with English, which permits up to four (Roach 2009: 59–60). Setter (2008a) shows that there are no Hong Kong English syllables with more than two consonants in the coda, although three-consonant onsets are attested. As mentioned above, diphthongs are treated as vowel + coda, where the coda is a glide (Cheung 1986: 29). If there is a diphthong, the glide is considered to have fulfilled the position of coda, and therefore no further consonant is permitted. This will have an effect on syllables in which a diphthong is followed by one or more consonants, as discussed in section 2.7. We will return to the discussion of syllables and syllable structure in Cantonese when we look at Hong Kong English speech rhythm in section 2.16.

2.11 The vowel inventory

Using the lexical sets developed by Wells (1982), and based on observations by Hung (2000) and Deterding et al. (2008), Table 2.3 presents the vowels of Hong Kong English.

Bolton and Kwok (1990) note that American English accent features also occur in Hong Kong English. Amongst speakers with features of an American accent, there may be some differences in NURSE, lettER, START, FORCE, NORTH, SQUARE, CURE, NEAR and POOR vowels, which can have varying amounts of r-colouring. That this feature is not stable is evident from Speakers 1 and 8. Speaker 1's lettER vowel in the second syllable of *after* is not r-coloured, but his NURSE vowel in *turn* is. Speaker 8 produces *her* with r-colouring, but her lettER vowel in *after* is also not r-coloured.

(45) after [ɑftə] you have reached springboks um you should um . . . turn [tɝn] left

{01-MT:01:22}

(46) I went there to visit her [hɚ] . . . because at that time [tɑm] it was after [ɑftə] graduation so I've got [gɔt] about three months' holiday [hɔlədeɪ]

{08-HE:00:22}

Table 2.3 The vowel inventory of Hong Kong English

FLEECE	i	NURSE	ɜ	GOAT	oʊ	GOOSE	u
KIT	i	lettER	ə	THOUGHT	ɔ	FOOT	u
happy	i	commA	ə	FORCE	ɔ	PRICE	aɪ
FACE	eɪ	START	ɑ	NORTH	ɔ	MOUTH	aʊ
DRESS	ɛ	PALM	ɑ	LOT	ɔ	CHOICE	ɔɪ
TRAP	ɛ	BATH	ɑ	CLOTH	ɔ	NEAR	ɪə
SQUARE	ɛə	STRUT	ʌ	CURE	ʊə	POOR	ʊə

Similarly, the BATH vowel in *after* in the examples above is [ɑ] rather than [æ], and the LOT vowel in *springboks*, *got* and *holiday* is [ɔ] rather than [ɑ], the latter in each case being the quality expected in American English, and found in the speech of some Hong Kong English speakers (Bolton and Kwok 1990: 154; Bradshaw 1997). American English influence is on the increase in Hong Kong. Luke and Richards, in 1982, indicate that the British accent is the most usual one for Hong Kong Chinese to emulate (Luke and Richards 1982: 55); by 1990, Bolton and Kwok note that the use of General American features had increased, and seem to suggest that this is a conscious choice amongst speakers (Bolton and Kwok 1990: 167). Bradshaw (1997) claims that it is not so much a matter of conscious choice between British and American English as speakers are able to draw on both varieties as and when they are exposed to them, which results in a mixed accent.

2.12 Vowel quality and quantity

It is possible to see from Table 2.3 that vowels often described as being in long and short pairs in RP are given the same symbol in Hong Kong English, indicating that there is no phonemic length difference. FLEECE and KIT, LOT and THOUGHT, and GOOSE and FOOT are represented with /i/, /ɔ/ and /u/ respectively. Figure 2.3 is a plot of the vowel monophthongs of Hong Kong English for the fifteen subjects in Hung's study (Hung 2000: 342), which shows that vowels in each of these three pairs are, in fact, very close to each other in quality, as are DRESS and TRAP. This chart differs somewhat from that of Deterding et al. (2008: 162), which indicates that GOOSE/FOOT are much further forward than LOT/THOUGHT, and also that neither pair is very close together. According to Hung (2000), there is no perceptible difference in length between FLEECE and

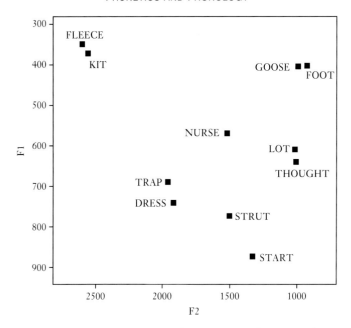

Figure 2.3 Average formant chart for fifteen subjects (Hung 2000)

KIT vowels in this variety, although length differences are perceptible in GOOSE and FOOT and LOT and THOUGHT. Deterding et al. (2008: 162) suggest that LOT and THOUGHT may not be merged at all.

Listening to our speakers, there is considerable individual and group variation in the production of the KIT vowel. Speaker 5, for example, sometimes produces KIT with a vowel nearer to the RP production, [ɪ], and sometimes with a merged vowel:

(47) don't get there ... there's still a- distant [dɪstɐnt]

{05-MT:04:36}

(48) and then can you see a rope bridge [brɪdʒ]

{05-MT:04:46}

In example (48) above, *bridge* is produced with a certain amount of lengthening; phrase-final lengthening is to be expected, but it is not as exaggerated in Hong Kong English as it is in Singapore English (Deterding 2007). Focusing on *bridge*, Speaker 8 uses [ɪ], but Speaker 10 has something more intermediate between [i] and [ɪ] (transcribed here as [i]):

(49) and then at some point you will see a rope bridge [brɪdʒ] on the east
{08-MT:03:31}

(50) but can you see the . . . rope bridge [brɪdʒ]
{10-MT:03:13}

When the KIT/FLEECE vowel occurs word-initially in Hong Kong English, there may be a palatal glide leading into it. Speaker 9 demonstrates this in his production of *easy*:

(51) and like sport game . . . yeah which is easy [jisi]
{09-HE:07:22}

Turning to pairs GOOSE/FOOT: one of the interesting features of this vowel pair is the fact that they may be somewhat fronted (Deterding et al. 2008), as in modern RP, but unlike in other varieties in the region, such as Singapore English (Deterding 2007: 24). Although this is not obvious from looking at Figure 2.3, which was generated from Hung's (2000) study in which he used word lists to collect the data, our speakers demonstrate GOOSE fronting quite clearly in the words *too* in extract (52), *grew* (53), *flew* (54), *beautiful* (55) and *amusement* (56), shown here with the symbol [ʉ].

(52) but still yeah I sometimes I I get Legos too [tʉ]
{01-HE:04:42}

(53) the fish grew [gɹʉ] really really fast
{05-HE:04:19}

(54) but time flew [flʉ] and I had to come back to Hong Kong
{08-HE:04:19}

(55) while we arrive we can see a very beautiful [bjʉtifo] environment
{09-HE:01:06}

(56) and that amusement [amjʉsmɛn] park was called . . . Lee Yuen
{10-HE:00:21}

2.13 Diphthongs

A characteristic feature of the GOAT diphthong in Hong Kong English is the first element, which is much further back than that of RP, and represented above as /oʊ/. This quality can be exemplified by Speaker 1's production of *know* and *so*:

(57) I I was just being you know so [soʊ] fascinated about you know [noʊ]
{01-HE:00:44}

It was noted above (section 2.7) that diphthongs are produced by
speakers in certain ways when a consonant follows. In the production
of centring diphthongs /ɪə/, /ɛə/ and /ʊə/ in open syllables, the diphthong may be produced as two distinct syllables, as in this example of
here from Speaker 10, where [.] is used to mark the syllable boundary:

(58) so it's no longer here [hi.ə]
{10-HE:00:29}

Speakers may also use a much more open vowel in place of the second
element in such diphthongs, which would result in, for example, *here*
being produced as [hi.ɐ]. Unfortunately there are no examples of this
in the data.

Hung (2000) postulates that there is a split of the /aɪ/ diphthong into
two, [aɪ] and [ʌɪ]. He demonstrates that only [aɪ] can occur in open
syllables, whereas both [aɪ] and [ʌɪ] occur in closed ones in his data.
However, he is unable to demonstrate a clear pattern either of allo-
phonic complementary distribution or of phonemic contrast in closed
syllables, and from this we deduce that the distribution in closed syllables is not context-dependent.

2.14 Word stress

Suprasegmental aspects of Hong Kong English – word stress, speech
rhythm and features of intonation – have not had as much attention in
the research literature as segmental aspects. It is beyond the scope of
this book to cover the area in detail, but here we explore some of the
more characteristic features of these aspects of English in Hong Kong,
starting with word stress.

There are occasional word stress patterns in the variety which stand
out. One such feature is the stressing of the penultimate syllable in words
ending with *-ative*, such as *communicative*, which may be pronounced as
[kəmjuniˈkeɪtɪv], rather than /kəˈmjuːnɪkətɪv/ in RP (see Hung 2005).
Some examples of similar stressing, albeit with a different suffix, are Speaker
1's production of *fascinated* in extract (59), and Speaker 5's *separated* (60),
which have similar stressing (the stress is indicated here with capitals):

(59) I I was just being you know so fasciNAted
{01-HE:00:43}

(60) so we sepaRAted the fish into different areas

{05-HE:02:41}

A plausible suggestion might be that the words are pronounced with this stress pattern by analogy with *fascination* and *separation*, in which the stress is on the penultimate syllable, and has therefore been incorrectly transferred to these related items by the speakers. Interestingly, however, Speaker 1 reverses the pattern in *decorations*, which has stress on the penultimate syllable in varieties like RP owing to the pre-stressed suffix *-tion*, but not in this speaker's production:

(61) we got something new DECorations christmas DECorations

{01-HE:01:51}

The verb *decorate* also appears in this passage, and is also stressed on the first syllable.

Giving words ending with the pre-stressed suffix *-ic* as an example, Hung (2005) shows that the effect of metrical structure may generate words such as *photographic* and *energetic* correctly, as such words have two distinct feet which start on a stressed syllable (that is, *ENerGETic* and *PHOtoGRAPHic*). In the case of *angelic*, however, the stress is assigned to the first syllable (*ANgelic*) and not the penultimate syllable (*anGELic*) by his participants, as the word is not metrically regular, beginning as it does with an unstressed syllable; the same effect is shown for *terrific* (*TERrific*) and *acidic* (*ACidic*). Metric regularity may explain the position of the main stress in *fasciNAted* and *sepaRAted*, or Speaker 1's production of *DECorations*, but it does not explain why the main stress in these words is positioned where it is. Extracts (59) and (60) could be explained by syllable weight, however (Hung 2005). Giving the examples *informative* and *communicative*, both stressed on the penultimate syllable by his speakers (*inforMAtive*, *communiCAtive*), Hung suggests that these syllables are stressed because they are heavy, in that they contain the vowel /eɪ/. This may account for *fasciNAted* and *sepaRAted*, as the penultimate syllable certainly contains this same heavy vowel nucleus. Syllable weight does not seem to account for Speaker 1's production of *decorations*, however, where the same vowel appears in the penultimate syllable.

Other stress puzzles include Speaker 5's production of *cartoons*, in which the main stress is on the first syllable in extract (62), with no evidence of context bringing on a possible stress-shift:

(62) we saw CARtoons when we were young

{05-HE:13:52}

The main stress in Speaker 9's *mosquito* also falls on the first syllable (this could be explained by Hung's metric regularity):

(63) peoples are always afraid of MOSquito

{09-HE:04:37}

Our suggestion is that, as many English nouns are stressed on the first syllable, the speakers have adopted that as a rule for stress assignment in *decorations, cartoons* and *mosquito*. What these data do suggest, along with those of Hung (2005) and also Wong (1991), is that it is not simply the case that the speakers have learned the word incorrectly at the time of lexical acquisition, but that they are applying their own rules of word stress to it.

In terms of how the stressing is realised from the point of view of pitch, it may be useful to look to Cantonese. Cantonese does not have lexical stress, but does have lexical tone; this tone is an integral part of the meaning of the syllable. In fact, Cantonese is thought to be one of the most complex of Chinese tone languages, in that it is considered by linguists to have between six and nine phonemically distinct tones, whereas Putonghua – normally thought of as the standard dialect – has four; Bauer and Benedict (1997: 118) list ten tones in Cantonese: High Level, High Falling, High Stopped, High Rising, Mid Level, Mid Stopped, Mid-Low Level, Mid-Low Falling, Mid-Low Rising and Mid-Low Stopped; but then they go on to say that most Hong Kong Cantonese speakers do not distinguish between the High Falling and High Level tones. The Stopped tones are usually grouped with the Level tones and considered to be 'allotones', as they occur on syllables which end with an unreleased plosive (or stop) consonant; as these syllables are much shorter in duration than those which do not end with a plosive, Stopped tones are therefore truncated or 'stopped' in comparison with the corresponding Level tone (see Bauer and Benedict 1997: 137–8). The tones are usually assigned numbers, as follows: High Level/Falling is 1; High Rising is 2; Mid Level is 3; Mid-Low Falling is 4; MidLow Rising is 5; Mid-Low Level is 6. It is usual to give the number of the tone immediately following the Romanised transcription of the syllable, so *mai5* is the syllable [mai] with a Mid-Low Rising tone on it, meaning *buy*, and *mai6* is the same syllable with a Mid-Low Level tone on it, meaning *sell*.

Luke (2008) considers word and sentence stress in Hong Kong English in terms of the three Cantonese tones L, H and L!, where L is a Low Level tone, H is a High Level tone and L! is a Mid-Low Falling tone. Luke suggests that syllables in Hong Kong English perceived to be prominent are assigned a high tone by speakers, with all preceding syllables assigned low tones, and all following syllables assigned low falling tones. Thus, *consider* is LHL!, *physical* is HL!L!, and *encyclopaedia* is LLLHL!L! in Hong Kong English (Luke 2008). There is then an inter-syllabic rule by which a low falling tone may be realised as a high tone if surrounded by other high tones, so *overhead projector* may be produced as HL!H LHL! or HHH LHL! (Luke 2008). As there are no word-list data in the recordings we collected, it is difficult to ascertain whether these patterns are being imposed on words by our speakers. However, in extracts (59), (60) and (61), *fascinated* and *separated* could be analysed as LLHL!, and *decorations* could be analysed as HL!L!L!.

2.15 Compound stress

Another typical feature of lexical stress in Hong Kong English is to do with noun compounds; for example, *blackbird*, *fruit cake* and *battery charger*. In varieties such as RP, the general rule is that the main stress is assigned to the first element in noun compounds, unless the second element is made of the first element; thus a *blackbird* is not 'a bird made of black' (female blackbirds are, in fact, brown), but a *cheese sandwich* is 'a sandwich made of cheese'. *Blackbird* is stressed on the first element, whereas *cheese sandwich* is stressed on the first syllable of the second element. There are, of course, exceptions to this; a *fruit cake* is 'a cake made of fruit', but is stressed on the first element. In addition, there are stress differences between RP and other varieties such as General American. In Hong Kong English, however, compound stress does not seem to exist with any consistency, with all speakers in the data almost unilaterally stressing the second element of a noun compound as if it were simply a noun with a premodifier. There are several noun compounds in the map task data, amongst them *diamond mine*, *(highest) view point* and *banana tree*, which are stressed as follows in RP: *DIAmond mine*, *(highest) VIEW point*, *baNAna tree*. Here are some examples from our speakers, with the main stress in capitals:

(64) erm can you see a diamond MINE next to you

{05-MT:00:00}

(65) mmm first you have to go north and on your left hand side you will see a diamond MINE

{08-MT:00:00}

(66) in front of you can you see the diamond MINE

{10-MT:00:00}

(67) um can you see a highest view POINT

{05-MT:01:02}

(68) and then you will be walking towards the highest view POINT

{08-MT:01:29}

(69) and can you see ... the highest view POINT

{10-MT:01:03}

(70) can you can you see um ... a banana TREE

{05-MT:03:23}

(71) follow that road and you will see the banana TREE

{08-MT:02:34}

(72) you can see a banana TREE ... can you see it

{10-MT:02:23}

In each case, the main stress in the compound falls on the last word, which is similar to the pattern found in premodifier + noun combinations in varieties such as British and American English.

2.16 Rhythm

Speech rhythm in varieties of English such as RP and General American is very often referred to as 'stress-timed' (or 'stress-based'), which means that the timing between the onsets of stressed syllables is roughly similar; this is as opposed to 'syllable-timed' (or 'syllable-based'), in which the timing between the onset of each syllable is roughly similar. Although this distinction has been dismissed in various studies looking at speech production (see, for example, Roach 1982 and Dauer 1983), the terms 'stress-timed' and syllable-timed' continue to be used as a kind of shorthand, particularly in English Language Teaching materials, to describe the perceived rhythmic patterns of various languages, or to place them on a continuum.

Cantonese, the first language (L1) of speakers of Hong Kong English, is described as 'an example of a language with syllable-timed rhythm' (Bauer and Benedict 1997: 316), in which, unlike English, each syllable receives a similar emphasis. This, according to Bauer and Benedict (1997), is closely related to the fact that all syllables have lexical tone in Cantonese. It is noted that a small number of syllables may receive a somewhat lighter stress but still retain their tones, but from the few examples given by Bauer and Benedict (1997) these appear to be the exception rather than the rule. However, the structure of the syllable in

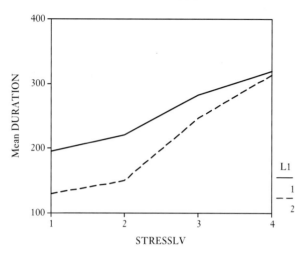

Figure 2.4 Line plot of syllable duration according to stress level for Hong Kong English and British English (Setter 2006)

Cantonese (described in section 2.10 above) means that some syllables, that is, those ending in a syllable-final plosive consonant, are considerably shorter than others, and this clearly has an effect on Hong Kong English.

If we review the syllable types which are available to a Cantonese speaker, we find that there are four, where the glide of a phonetic diphthong is included in C_f following Bauer and Benedict (1997): V, VC_f, C_iV, C_iVC_f. As there are also syllabic nasals in Cantonese, which carry tone movement – mid-low falling [m] (*no, not*) and mid-low rising [ŋ] (*five*) – we can also say that C_{syl} is a possible syllable in Cantonese, bringing the total to five. As it has been mentioned that only a few syllables may weaken but still retain their tone, it can be surmised that the vast majority of syllables in Cantonese will have a full vowel of one kind or another. This would indicate that Cantonese is a syllable-timed rather than stress-timed language.

Where, then, is Hong Kong English on the stress- vs. syllable-timed continuum?

Setter (2006) compared the duration of weakened, unstressed, stressed and nuclear syllables in Hong Kong English and British English, finding that Hong Kong English speakers do not shorten weakened and unstressed syllables to the same extent as British English speakers. Figure 2.4 is a graphical representation of this finding, in which Hong Kong English is given as 1 (solid line) and British English as 2 (dashed line); stress level 1 is weakened, level 2 is unstressed, level 3 is stressed and level 4 is nuclear; mean duration is shown in milliseconds.

What is clear from this diagram is that there is some maintenance of difference in duration between the various stress levels in Hong Kong English, albeit not as markedly as in British English. However, when one takes into account the proportion of weakened syllables as opposed to unstressed syllables, the picture is quite different. In the Hong Kong English sample, there was a much lower incidence of weak syllables (containing schwa or another permitted weak syllable nucleus) than unstressed syllables (containing a full vowel), with weak syllables accounting for 19.3 per cent of all those produced and unstressed syllables accounting for 43.64 per cent. By comparison, in the British English sample, weak syllables made up the greatest proportion (34.81 per cent), with the next highest being unstressed (26.96 per cent). There were similar proportions of stressed (Hong Kong English 21.8 per cent, BRE 22.09 per cent) and nuclear syllables (Hong Kong English 15.28 per cent, BRE 16.13 per cent) for both groups. This being the case, Hong Kong English may be perceived as syllable-timed due to the maintenance of full vowels in non-prominent syllables in combination with the less marked differences in duration between stressed and unstressed syllables in comparison with varieties such as British English. A further study which compared the length of the vowel in successive syllables (Setter 2008b) indicated that Hong Kong English is somewhere between British and Singapore English (as measured by Low et al. 2000) on the stress- vs. syllable-timed continuum.

What also needs to be mentioned is that speech rhythm varies not only between speakers of different language groups, but also within them, dependent on the speaker and on the speech event. Speech rhythm in varieties such as British and American English can vary from the highly stress-timed (for example, in rap music) to the rather more syllable-timed in situations where the speaker wishes to place emphasis on each syllable, or where the utterance simply lacks obvious weak syllables (for example, *birds eat worms*). This being the case, the extracts which follow demonstrate a Hong Kong English speaker with a somewhat syllable-timed rhythm (Speaker 10), followed by another with a more stress-timed rhythm (Speaker 1). In the first example (73), there is a clear lack of weakening of vowels in unstressed syllables (*for, a, and*), whereas in the second (74), it is more variable.

(73) we n- normally stay there for a whole day . . . and we enjoyed our time
there [wi n̩ nɔməli steɪ dɛə fɔr eɪ hoʊ deɪ . . . ɛn wi ɛndʒɔɪd ɑ tɑm ðɛə]
{10-HE:01:02}

(74) cause we went to London and there's like loads of um kids inside and they got Legos and other kind of things [kəz wi wɛnt tə lʌndən ɛn deəz laik loʊdz ɒv ʌm kɪdz ɪnsaɪd ɛn deɪ gɑt lɛgoʊz ən ʌðə kaɪnd əv θɪŋz]

{01-HE:05:12}

2.17 Sentence stress

Sentence stress in Hong Kong English is characterised by the main stress, or nucleus, being consistently located on the last word, with no attempt to move it to de-accent repeated items or highlight those requiring emphasis or to indicate contrast (Bolton and Kwok 1990: 154–161; Deterding et al. 2008). In our data, examples of lack of de-accenting of repeated items are shown in extract (75), where Speaker 9 fails to de-accent *mine*, and in (76), where Speaker 5 fails to de-accent *point*, even though she has already referred to the *highest view point* more than once before.

(75) 09:   so we are at the starting point and do you see the diamond mine
        [. . .]
     Int: yeah I see the diamond mine yep
     09:   yes you see so um now go south until you pass the diamond MINE

{09-MT:00:01}

(76) 05:   can you see a highest viewpoint
     Int: yes there is one yes there's one on . . . er well towards the north east direction of where I am
        [. . .]
     05:   that's right so um . . . um the springboks actually is before the highest viewPOINT on your left
        [. . .]
     Int: so where shall I go now
     05:   and then um you should um go past the highest viewPOINT fr- from the back of it

{05-MT:01:02}

An example of contrastive stress is given by Speaker 9 when he talks about urban and rural areas in Hong Kong; *urban* and *rural* should be the focus for contrast, but instead he highlights *area* in both cases.

(77) there more there are more rural ARea than than urban ARea

{09-HE:05:33}

However, it is not the case that speakers always put their nucleus on the last word in an utterance.

Another feature is the tendency of speakers to highlight personal pronouns unexpectedly (Deterding et al. 2008). In extract (78), Speaker 8 emphasises *me* where there is no contrast with another speaker; in (79), Speaker 9 emphasises *me* even though this is a repetition of reference to himself; and in (80), Speaker 10 emphasises *you* rather than *closer*, which is the last content word (although these last two examples are consistent with the tendency to stress the last word).

(78)   let ME talk about my trip to Canada

{08-HE:00:03}

(79)   Int: were you alone I mean er with other kids . . . or were you was
               your mother with you
       09:    oh yes my mother . . . is always with ME

{09-HE:03:25}

(80)   there should be another one that's closer to YOU

{10-MT:02:02}

2.18 Pitch and nuclear tones

Until recently, there has been very little work indeed on pitch and nuclear tones in Hong Kong English. Bolton and Kwok (1990), for example, only have a paragraph on suprasegmental features in the variety. They assert that speakers tend to use a rising intonation on all question types, including wh-questions, and show in their displays of the pitch contour that statements often have a fall on them (Bolton and Kwok 1990: 154–60). Most other works on Hong Kong English do not treat this area at all. The exception is Cheng et al. (2008), which is a comprehensive non-acoustic study of discourse intonation in a corpus of Hong Kong English. Here, we look at some of the patterns which arise in our data, but we caution that this is not intended to be a full treatment of pitch patterns in the variety.

As mentioned above, the nucleus tends to be on the last word in a sentence or clause. On the whole, the speakers use a range of nuclear tones in their speech, including all those covered in Cruttenden (2008): high fall and low fall; high rise and low rise; fall-rise; rise-fall; and level. In our map task data, we found that the highest-incidence tone was the level tone (43.32 per cent) – as observed also in Cheng et al.'s corpus (2008: 126) – followed by the rise (24.39 per cent), the fall (23.02 per cent), the fall-rise (8.68 per cent) and finally the rise-fall (0.59 per cent).

The rise-fall, a strongly dominant tone which can indicate indignation, sarcasm or, conversely, being surprised or very impressed by something (Cruttenden 2008: 284), is very low incidence in the data, as it was in Cheng et al.'s corpus. In the small number of instances in which it is used in our recordings, it has none of the meanings associated with it by Cruttenden (2008). In Singapore English, the rise-fall is often used to indicate extra emphasis (Deterding 2007: 37). Here are some examples from our recordings, in which the speakers are not indignant, sarcastic, surprised or impressed; the rise-fall is shown by '↗↘'. Speaker 5 could be indicating extra emphasis in extract (81), but this explanation seems unlikely in Speaker 10's extract (82):

(81)　and then . . . er after that you can see the finish point . . . on your right and you can see me ↗↘there

{05-MT:06:23}

(82)　and ↗↘then . . . um . . . on your left hand side

{10-MT:02:15}

As mentioned above, Bolton and Kwok (1990) comment that all questions, including wh-questions, tend to end with a rise in Hong Kong English. Cheng et al.'s (2008) findings, however, along with that of Lin (2008), show this not to be the case. There are not many instances of wh-questions in our data, but here are two examples of questions in reported speech from Speaker 5 where she uses a rise or fall-rise rather than a fall.

(83)　he ↘↗ask me um ↘↗((name)) what do you usually ↘↗order for ↘↗food during you dinner ↗time

{05-HE:07:17}

(84)　↗what what do you ↗mean

{05-HE:08:04}

There is an interesting use of intonation by several speakers on the phrase *and then*, in which is it produced with a rising pitch on *then* when used as a lead into another phrase or sentence. This seems to be a phrasal pattern specific to this sequence of words. Speakers 9 and 10 use this pattern quite regularly in the map task recordings.

(85)　and ↗then you turn to . . . er then you go east

{09-MT:00:23}

(86) yeah and ↗then you will you will be ah at the foot of the mountain and ↗then you keep going north and just um when you see . . . ah you you pass the mountain and ↗then you turn east again
{09-MT:01:19}

(87) and ↗then you will possibly see a field station
{09-MT:02:11}

(88) and ↗then keep going
{10-MT:01:28}

(89) and ↗then um . . . in the in in the direction of north of you
{10-MT:03:54}

In some accents of English, including Australian, New Zealand and younger speakers in the UK, there is a tendency towards a phenomenon known as 'upspeak' or 'uptalk' (see Bradford 1997; Cruttenden 1997: 129–30; Wells 2006: 37–8). This is where the intonation rises at the end of declaratives (shown by '↗') rather than falling (shown by '↘'). Cruttenden (2008) suggests that this might be to ensure the listener is paying attention, because a rising tone often requires some kind of response from the listener. There are examples of upspeak in our data from all five speakers. Here are examples of declaratives with a falling tone and a rising tone for each speaker. In the first example (90), we can also see Speaker 1 using rising tones to indicate he has not finished his turn yet.

(90) 01:   when I was a ↗kid erm around the age of erm ↗ten
     Int: ten years
     01:   eleven around and mmm I actually I studied in er in the same primary school with my ↘brother
{01-HE:00:00}

(91) I I was just being you know so fascinated about you know . . . to to be a ↗kid again I'll say you know in a way like compared to ↗now
{01-HE:00:56}

(92) because I used to study in a very prestigious school in Hong ↘Kong
{05-HE:06:56}

(93) well I got a quite interesting ↗childhood
{05-HE:00:00}

(94) let me talk about my trip to ↘Canada
{08-HE:00:03}

(95)　and we . . . spent about four days there because I've never been to Vancouver be⬈fore

{08-HE:00:48}

(96)　the church organise a a wild camp ac⬊tivities

{09-HE:00:20}

(97)　Int:　so er all in all you stayed how how long did you stay there
09:　um I I just stay there for one ⬈night

{09-HE:02:27}

(98)　10:　and my father bring er brought me to er some amusement ⬊park
Int:　amusement park yeah
10:　yeah and there's one quite near to my ⬊house

{10-HE:00:09}

(99)　um I think around . . . once a ⬈month or once every ⬈two months because it's very close to my ⬈home

{10-HE:01:09}

2.19 Summary

This chapter has looked at phonological patterns in Hong Kong English, and has shown that there are identifiable features common to its speakers in terms of vowel and consonant realisation and of patterns observed in consonant cluster production, and also in suprasegmental features such as word and sentence stress, speech rhythm and intonation. There has been some discussion of these features in the light of the phonology of Cantonese and, although many features could be seen as a result of the interaction between English and Cantonese, there are some, such as the addition of extra final consonants, which do not seem to be the result of this interaction. In the next chapter, we consider morphological and grammatical structures.

Note

1. We again refer readers to the Linguistics Society of Hong Kong (LSHK) website, which houses the description of the LSHK Romanisation Scheme (mainly in Chinese), at the following link: http://www.lshk.org/cantonese.php.

3 Morphosyntax

As is the case with phonology, many of the morphosyntactic features in Hong Kong English reflect the interaction between English and Cantonese, two languages very different in terms of their morphological and grammatical structures.

Like other Chinese dialects, Cantonese is not morphologically rich. There are few inflectional and derivational markings in Cantonese (Matthews and Yip 1994: 31). When compared to English, Cantonese has no tense inflections on the verbs; nor are there any number or gender inflections on the nouns. As a result, the English morphological markings are realised in four different ways in Hong Kong English. One typical feature is the simplification of the English morphology (Budge 1989). For example, the suffix -*s* is omitted from verbs with third person singular subjects, as in 'he give all the picture to you; he like de boy better den de girl' (Platt 1982: 409). The second is the optional use of suffixes such as the -*s* for plural nouns. For example, in the sentence 'where de movie all come from' (Platt 1982: 409), the noun 'movie' is not marked for plural. In the noun phrase 'many gardens and many famous place' there are two noun phrases each headed by a plural noun. However, the first plural noun has the suffix -*s* while the second one does not. Third, the past tense is not marked, either. Platt (1982: 410) has the following examples reporting past events: 'Mandarin, I learn it privately' and 'I don't learn at secondary school'. The fourth morphological feature that typifies Hong Kong English is morphologically doubly marked items such as 'more better' or 'more richer'.

In grammar, a similar phenomenon distinguishes Hong Kong English from Standard English – it is influenced by Cantonese. While subject-less sentences are found in Hong Kong English, double subjects are also widespread. The following two examples, the first from Poon (2006: 26) and the second from McArthur (2002: 361), illustrate exactly this point: 'Sorry! HK$500 & $1000 not accept' (the subject 'we' is omitted) and 'Passengers who take the ferry service from Ma Liu Shui, they can enjoy a free ride from Tap Mun to Wong Shek' (on a notice; the subject 'they' in the second clause is extra). These two characteristics result directly from two major Cantonese grammatical features which have obviously influenced Hong Kong English. The first grammatical property is that Cantonese permits subjectless sentences, especially when the subject of the sentence is a pronoun. Standard English, on the other hand, does not allow a zero subject co-occurring with a tensed verb. Sentences like 'Comes home around six every day' are common in Hong Kong English but rare in Standard English.

The other typological difference between English and Cantonese is that Cantonese tends to be a topic-prominent language.[1] This probably leads to the production of English sentences with an apparent subject noun phrase which is, in fact, not the grammatical subject but the topic of the discourse. For example, the following conversation is quite likely to occur between two Hongkongers:

A: Do you think he has this book?
B: Yes, this book, has. (=Yes, he has this book.)

In the dialogue above, the noun phrase *this book* is the topic of the discourse initiated by Speaker A. In B's utterance, *this book* is the topic which links his response to A's question; it is not the grammatical subject of the sentence. What further complicates the issue here is the fact that Cantonese also allows subjectless sentences, especially if the subject is a pronoun. In this case, the subject in B's response is *he*, which is omitted. As a result of these two grammatical features, topic-prominence and subjectless sentences, the noun phrase *this book* thus appears to be the subject in B's response but the real subject, *he*, is in fact omitted.

In other cases, when the grammatical subject is not omitted, double subjects are frequently found in Hong Kong English speakers' speech. For example, in 'my mother, she likes to watch TV', the first noun phrase *my mother* is the topic while the second noun phrase, the pronoun *she*, is the real grammatical subject. Although the two noun phrases have the same reference, it is not common in Standard English to mark the topic by a single noun phrase when the grammatical subject immediately follows it. However, such a grammatical structure of 'topic NP – S', where NP refers to the noun phrase and S refers to the subject of a sentence, is very common in Hong Kong English. As a result of the interaction between English and Cantonese, both subjectless and double-subject sentences are very common in Hong Kong English.

These, and other issues, are discussed in this chapter.

3.1 'Random' morphological markings

As mentioned in the previous section, morphology in Hong Kong English is either simplified or doubly marked. Inflectional suffixation is where these two features are most visible. Both features can be found within a single speaker as well as across speakers.

One of the inflectional suffixes that evidently marks Hong Kong English from Standard English is the suffix -*s* (for plural nouns as well as for verbs with a third person singular subject). On the surface, it appears that the use of the plural suffix -*s* is random in Hong Kong English.[2] A more in-depth analysis demonstrates that at least three distinctive features contribute to this apparently random morphological marking of plurality.

The first, most common feature among speakers of Hong Kong English is the use of a singular count noun in its bare form. In Standard English, a singular count noun will either be preceded by an article, *a*, *an* or *the*, or it will be in the plural form with generic reference. In Hong Kong English, the bare form of a noun is normally used for generic reference regardless of whether the noun is a count noun or a mass noun. The examples below illustrate this point well.

(1) yes and you see ... there there will be <u>giraffe</u>

{09-MT:03:30}

(2) but the fact is um so people is always peoples are always afraid of <u>mosquito</u> some insects

{09-HE:04:32}

This feature is obviously not simply a morphological issue of the non-marking of plural nouns because, in the two examples above, some nouns have indeed been marked for plural; for example, *insects* and *peoples*. The use of *giraffe* in extract (1) and *mosquito* in (2) thus reveals more of a systemic grammatical feature of Hong Kong English in which a singular count noun is used in its bare form without any prenominal modification. This relates to the non-distinction between count and non-count nouns in Hong Kong English. This feature will be revisited in section 3.6 on noun phrases.

The second feature is a bona fide morphological feature. In Hong Kong English, the omission of the -*s* suffix in plural nouns is commonplace. The following examples from our corpus illustrate this feature.

(3) but I think it's very interesting maybe because of these <u>kind</u> of <u>thing</u>

{05-HE:06:36}

(4) but but I'm glad that I've got <u>all these experience</u>

{05-HE:10:14}

(5) all <u>sort</u> of dangerous things

{05-HE:13:29}

(6) yes um so we have like ten <u>family</u>

{09-HE:04:01}

(7) snakes er . . . yes . . . um . . . and I think people do not want to bother too many <u>thing</u> because

{09-HE:04:45}

(8) but they are very <u>small scale one</u> for children

{10-HE:01:34}

In the six examples above, the plural marker -*s* is omitted from all the head nouns in the noun phrases. These examples are different from the ones quoted earlier. In extracts (1) and (2), the head nouns are the only element in the noun phrase, without any modifications. However, in examples (3) to (8), the grammatical cue for plurality is very strong: most of the head nouns are immediately preceded by a plural determiner: *these* in (3) and (4), *all* in (5), *ten* in (6), *many* in (7) and the reference of *one* to the subject *they* in (8). This is contrary to Budge's suggestion that 'Hong Kong English speakers tend to mark plural where there is some semantic reminder that the noun is to be marked as plural', particularly where the semantic reminder is 'stronger or more unambiguous' (Budge 1989: 41); in examples (3) to (8) above, the semantic reminder is definitely very strong because the modifier or reference which requires a plural head noun immediately precedes it, and yet these head nouns do not occur in their expected plural forms.

The third feature which contributes to the apparently random marking of plural nouns is the use of the plural suffix to mark singular count nouns. Below are some examples from our speakers.

(9) um your brother never got into <u>trouble</u> . . . you were always the one getting in <u>troubles</u>

{05-HE:12:04}

(10) because my <u>mothers</u> er he he er my mother she

{09-HE:00:12}

(11) so they are in <u>a very small scales</u> and yeah and also we ... we n- nor-
      mally stay there for a whole day

                                                    {10-HE:00:55}

(12) yes and then at the point when you see <u>a springboks</u>

                                                    {08-MT:00:53}

(13) and then you turn to er then you go east until you see <u>a springboks</u>

                                                    {09-MT:00:22}

(14) and then um ... <u>every children</u> they they came with their parents and
      actually <u>each tents</u> um is a unit for a family

                                                    {09-HE:03:50}

In summary, the description of the seemingly random plural marking
of nouns in Hong Kong English can be subcategorised into three types:
(a) singular count nouns are used in their bare form; (b) the plural suffix
is missing from plural nouns; and (c) the plural suffix is used to mark
singular nouns.

By the same token, the -*s* suffix on verbs which marks a third person
singular subject is often omitted (Platt 1982), but interestingly this suffix
is sometimes used with non-third person singular subjects. This random
morphological marking results in what appears to be a subject–verb
disagreement feature, as shown in the extracts below.

(15) and <u>the church organise</u> a a wild camp activities so

                                                    {09-HE:00:19}

(16) something <u>that never happen</u> in real life

                                                    {05-HE:14:01}

(17) er but it <u>it still take</u> like three to four hours to to go there ... aha

                                                    {09-HE:05:55}

(18) yeah ((laughs)) cause <u>they barks</u> a lot and

                                                    {05-HE:01:23}

(19) they pro <u>they provides</u> all the facilities like showering

                                                    {09-HE:07:16}

Added to the list of random morphological marking is the -*ed* suffix,
used to show the past tense and past participle on verbs. The omission
of the past tense suffix may in fact be a result of the tense-switching
phenomenon in Hong Kong English, which will be discussed in section
3.3 below. The following examples extracted from our data illustrate
the non-marking of the past participle.

(20) but it but it seems you know it's I <u>have pass</u> the the age of

{01-HE:05:03}

(21) no no no he's <u>he's just er climb</u> up and then jump er jumped

{05-HE:11:51}

(22) yeah I don't know what . . . <u>that's call</u>

{05-HE:14:21}

(23) ah . . . because they're well equipped they <u>have prepare</u> all the faci-
they pro they provides all the facilities like showering

{09-HE:07:12}

(24) advance and the the the because <u>it's um</u> . . . <u>subsidise</u> by the
government

{09-HE:07:29}

It can be concluded from examples (15) to (24) above that verbs in
Hong Kong English frequently lack the morphological markings that
usually mark verbs in Standard English.

3.2 Double morphological markings

While morphological markings seem to be optional and simplified in
Hong Kong English, one might wonder why double morphological
markings emerge at all. If we take a closer look at the morphology
of Standard English, we will find that while the majority of English
words have regular inflected forms (consider *book / books; walk /
walked / have walked; big / bigger / biggest*), a number of common nouns,
verbs and adjectives have an irregular inflected form (consider *child
/ children; go / went / gone; bad / worse / worst; beautiful / more beautiful
/ most beautiful*). Such variability, to a certain extent, may contribute
to double markings found in Hong Kong English. Although not very
frequent in our corpus, the few examples found indicate that double
morphological markings tend to have a close link to the irregular morphology of Standard English. The examples below well illustrate this
point:

(25) or other er more . . . um <u>more better</u> facilities

{09-HE:00:40}

(26) but I <u>didn't telled</u> him

{05-HE:09:38}

(27) sometimes she <u>would even took</u> me to the park to have roller blade . . .
um skating

{08-HE:00:59}

(28) so that's why I was very excited but um . . . it it takes so much time to
arrive to the camp camp site um and then I think it takes er . . . it <u>tooks</u>
er more than an hour travel by bus

{09-HE:00:46}

In example (25) above, the comparative form of the adjective *good* is
doubly marked by the use of *more* plus the irregular inflected form *better*.
In the verb group in example (26), both the auxiliary verb and the main
verb are marked for the past, and the irregular form of the verb *tell* is
'regularised' with the *-ed* suffix. Extract (27) is similar to (26) in that the
auxiliary verb *would* has already marked the past tense but the irregular
verb *took* is doubly marked for the past as well. The last example, *tooks*
in (28), is perhaps a slip-of-the-tongue error, but it presents another
piece of evidence that irregular forms tend to be more prone to diverse
usage.

These items, albeit idiosyncratic, reflect the fact that the irregularity
in morphology in Standard English plus the various grammatical opera-
tions which interact with the morphology lead to some features observable in Hong Kong English.

In the following sections, grammatical features specific to Hong Kong
English will be the focus.

3.3 Tense switching

McArthur (2002: 360) has commented that Hong Kong English speakers tend to use the present tense for all tenses (including past and
future) and the time reference is usually indicated by a time phrase.
Although in our data this is not exactly the case, it is evident that Hong
Kong English speakers do not show a great variety of verb tenses in
their speech. In most cases, only the past and the present tenses are
used, with a few cases in which the future tense[3] is employed. One
typical feature of Hong Kong English in terms of verb tense is 'tense
switching'. For example, in extract (29) below, the speaker is recount-
ing one of the happy events in his childhood; the first three verbs in
his utterance are in the present tense form (underlined) but suddenly
the last verb is in the past tense (double underlined) for no particular
reason.

(29) some people <u>win</u> some some <u>lose</u> and . . . er so after several hours so
      it's around noon time and then we <u>have</u> to go back so we <u>walk</u> another
      two hours and then one hour bus and . . . <u>came</u> back to the city
      {09-HE:02:06}

Such inconsistent use of tense, or the constant switching between the
past and the present tense, is quite common in Hong Kong English. A
similar phenomenon is found in Singapore English as well; Deterding
(2007: 46) suggests that there is a tendency for the speaker 'to switch
into the present tense when narrating a past event'.

Below are some more examples from our data. Extracts (30) to (35)
are from Speaker 1, who is describing what happened during the run-up
to Christmas when he was very young.

(30) when I <u>was</u> a kid . . . and . . . I actually <u>studied</u> and aah in the same
      primary school with my brother. . . and the last day before we <u>have</u> our
      Christmas holiday
      {01-HE:00:00}

(31) my dad usually <u>drive</u> his car and <u>pick</u> me up
      {01-HE:00:17}

(32) somewhere else so yeah he <u>drove</u> us there and then we we <u>spent</u> hours
      over there and <u>pick</u> something we <u>like</u> and usually I <u>discuss</u> with my
      brother and like aah you (coughs) how about you <u>get</u> this and I <u>get</u>
      that one and so we <u>can</u> you know <u>play</u> together
      {01-HE:01:07}

(33) we <u>got</u> something new decorations Christmas decorations . . . and after
      that aah we <u>will go</u> to Kentucky Fried Chicken which <u>is</u> right next to
      it because kids <u>love</u> fries and fried pan-fried stuff and so yeah my dad
      <u>would take</u> us there and we <u>eat</u> some kind of snacks you know before
      we <u>go</u> back home for dinner
      {01-HE:01:50}

(34) and we <u>can</u> we we <u>could touch</u> it but we <u>cannot open</u> it
      {01-HE:02:52}

(35) when I <u>was</u> smaller or around um . . . six to seven years old we usually
      <u>buy</u> Legos
      {01-HE:04:24}

The extracts quoted above are quite typical of Hong Kong English
speakers. If these six examples above are viewed as a coherent piece

and all the verbs are examined in greater detail in terms of the narrative relevant to the theme of Speaker 1's happy childhood days, it is obvious that the 'tense-switching' feature is very frequent for this speaker, as summarised in (36).

(36) *was* → *studied* → *have* ... → ... *drive* → *pick* ... → ... *drove* → *spent* → *pick* → *like* → *discuss* → *get* → *get* → *can* → *play* ... → ... *got* → *will go* → *is* → *love* ... → *would take* → *eat* → *go* ... → ... *can* → *could touch* → *cannot open* ... → ... *was* → *buy* ...

Deterding (2007: 47) takes the view that in Singapore English, 'it seems that use of past-tense forms of verbs is quite variable, even when narrating a story, and there is a pattern of slipping into the present tense as soon as the past time of the events has been established, especially for stative verbs and those describing something habitual'. Such an observation seems to be able to account for most of the cases of the use of the present tense in the examples above.

The following examples, extracted from Speaker 5, show a very similar feature, with higher frequency of tense switching than Speaker 1:

(37) 05:   some of them <u>looked</u> very sick
      Int: oh yeah
      05:   so we <u>move</u> them ((laughs)) to one partition this <u>is</u> the sick room
                                                            {05-HE:02:55}

(38) so we <u>use</u> to go there a lot and then what <u>happen</u> <u>was</u> the fish er <u>grew</u> really really fast
                                                            {05-HE:03:34}

(39) ((laughs)) cause erm like I actually <u>didn't understand</u> a lot of things that my classmate erm <u>talk</u> about
                                                            {05-HE:06:44}

(40) he <u>ask</u> me um ((name)) what <u>do</u> you usually <u>order</u> for food
                                                            {05-HE:07:17}

(41) oh like each of them <u>order</u> a food or . . . or like they <u>took</u> turns like today maybe
                                                            {05-HE:07:31}

(42) and then I think erm he <u>said</u> yesterday I <u>order</u> erm
                                                            {05-HE:08:05}

(43) I actually <u>broke</u> my forehead I <u>injure</u> it

{05-HE:10:27}

(44) 05:   no no he's he's just er <u>climb</u> up and then <u>jump</u> er <u>jumped</u>
      Int: to the floor yeah mhm mhm
      05:   and then I just <u>follow</u> cause

{05-HE:11:54}

(45) cause when we <u>were</u> young we <u>live</u> with our er grandfather

{05-HE:12:33}

(46) so he <u>got</u> a room my brother and I both <u>live</u> with my parents in one
      room

{05-HE:12:38}

The majority of the verbs used in the above narrative piece produced
by Speaker 5 are in the present tense while the rest are in the simple
past tense, as indicated in (47). The tense-switching feature mirrors the
pattern observed in Speaker 1 above. However, not all the verbs that are
in the present tense are stative verbs or refer to something habitual (e.g.
talk, jump, follow).

(47) *looked* → *move* → *is* ... → ... *use* → *happen* → *was* → *grew* ... → ... *didn't
      understand* → *talk* ... → ... *ask* → *do* ... *order* ... → ... *order* → *took* ... →
      ... *said* → *order* ... → ... *broke* → *injure* ... → ... *climb* → *jump* → *jumped*
      → *follow* ... → ... *were* → *live* ... → ... *got* → *live* ...*

In other words, Deterding's (2007) description of Singapore English
may only partially explain the frequent use of the present tense in Hong
Kong English. Individual variations may contribute to the overall difference between Singapore English and Hong Kong English.

The same pattern is also found among the other three speakers in the
data. Below are some more extracts.

(48) well there <u>were</u> a lot we <u>have</u> sushi ... seafood ... pasta

{08-HE:03:24}

(49) mhm ... ah she <u>was</u> not good at cooking because ... she <u>said</u> that she
      <u>does</u> not have any time to cook

{08-HE:03:54}

(50) so that's why I <u>was</u> very excited but um ... it it <u>takes</u> so much time to
      arrive to the camp camp site um and then I think it <u>takes</u> er ... it <u>tooks</u>
      er more than an hour travel by bus

{09-HE:00:46}

(51) er but it <u>was removed</u> now so it's no longer here so at that time I <u>went</u> there and . . . actually I <u>went</u> there with my brother and my father and we <u>enjoyed</u> our time there like we <u>play</u> some games

{10-HE:00:28}

(52) because er my father er it's it's that we <u>had</u> two of us so fath- my father <u>can</u> only take care of two of us <u>can</u> not like go with many young kids because it's too dangerous

{10-HE:03:45}

Below is another set of extracts showing more tense features in Hong Kong English. In addition to tense switching, another feature emerges from this set of data in which the past tense is used to mark a time reference which is non-present.

(53) yes I <u>stayed</u> in Hong Kong actually for my life before I came here

{08-HE:04:35}

(54) er especially . . . the weather in Hong Kong is quite hot so we always <u>kept</u> in a air con room

{09-HE:08:38}

(55) yeah ah you go south um you will see a diamond mine on your left hand side <u>did you see</u> it

{08-MT:00:34}

(56) yeah but don't go too far away from the banana tree where you'll see another field station so ah while you you <u>saw</u> the banana tree go south again

{09-MT:02:45}

In example (53), instead of using the present perfect tense *have stayed* to indicate duration up till the present moment, the speaker chooses to use the simple past tense. In example (54), it is plausible to interpret the past tense *kept* as meaning 'so we've always kept (ourselves) in a air con room'. Similarly, the past tense form of the verbs in the other two examples may be used to indicate the perfective aspect.

When all the above examples from (29) to (56) are viewed together, it is not difficult to conclude that one very characteristic Hong Kong English feature is the frequent tense switching between the present and past tenses. In some cases, the simple past tense is employed to indicate a non-present time.

At this point, it may be worthwhile to discuss the features of the

Table 3.1 Instances of the future tense in Hong Kong English

	Happy event		Map task		Total
	will	**would**	**will**	**would**	
Speaker 1	*we will go my mum will stay at home*	*my dad would take us*	*will be able*	0	4
Speaker 5	0	*you would pass through* *you wouldn't believe* *I would stop crying* *I would become* *I would follow* *we would play* *someone would sleep* *one of us would sleep*	*you will get*	0	9
Speaker 8	*you will get*	*I would go* *she would join* *we would go (2)* *she would take* *she would even took*	*you will see (8)* *you will be walking* *you will go (3)* *you will be going* *you will follow (2)* *will be*	0	23
Speaker 9	*you will possibly be*	0	*you will see* *you will be* *there will be* *you'll see*	0	5
Speaker 10	0	0	*you will see*	0	1
Total	4	15	23	0	42

future tense in Hong Kong English. In our data, a total of forty-two instances of future tenses are found (see Table 3.1).

Each of these instances is used to indicate some future event or events. In other words, while tense switching between the past and the present is quite common, in our data the future tense is not switched with the present or the past. However, in the few instances where it is found in the happy event task, the simple future tense is used instead of the 'future in the past' which is usually found in other varieties of English. For example:

(57) we got something new decorations Christmas decorations . . . and after that um we <u>will</u> go to . . . Kentucky Fried Chicken

{01-HE:01:50}

This echoes the past/present tense switching described above: the past future is replaced by the simple (present) future.

A major difference between Hong Kong English and Standard English observed from these forty-two examples is that the contracted form is rarely used by our speakers. Only one instance of *you'll* is found in the whole corpus. The future tense is exclusively realised with *will* and *would*.

To sum up this section on tense switching, we can conclude that Hong Kong English has a tense system of present versus past, realised in the verbs. These two tenses can sometimes be switched between without any intention of a change of perspective. On the other hand, the future tense, which is lexically marked by the auxiliary *will* or *would*, is seldom switched with either the present or past tense.

3.4 Subject–verb agreement

In the use of the present tense, number agreement between the subject and the verb is grammatically marked. Number in English grammar refers to the singular versus the plural, and this is realised both on the noun and on the verb group in terms of subject–verb agreement. In Hong Kong English, some speakers may show some inconsistency in marking verbs so that they do not agree in number with the third person subjects. Here are some examples from our data:

(58) and <u>the church organise</u> a a wild camp activities so

{09-HE:00:19}

(59) something <u>that never happen</u> in real life

{05-HE:14:01}

(60) er but it <u>it still take</u> like three to four hours to to go there . . . aha

{09-HE:05:55}

(61) the the <u>cows' faeces which is</u> very smelly

{09-HE:01:19}

(62) yeah ((laughs)) cause <u>they barks</u> a lot and

{05-HE:01:23}

(63) they pro <u>they provides</u> all the facilities like showering

{09-HE:07:16}

(64) and the hygiene quality ah the hygiene and <u>all the conditions is is</u> very nice

{09-HE:07:41}

(65) yes and ... but we ... er actually the geography Hong Kong is <u>there are more urban area</u> there more <u>there are more rural area</u> than than urban area

{09-HE:05:25}

Amongst the five speakers in our data, only the speech of two speakers (Speaker 5 and Speaker 9) shows some inconsistency in subject–verb agreement. The above examples are all those that can be found which show such an inconsistency. In other words, in most cases, subject–verb agreement is maintained in the same way as in Standard English. Examples (58) to (64) fall into two groups: (58) to (60) illustrate utterances in which the verb is not marked for a third person singular subject – the suffix -*s* is omitted from the verb. Examples (61) to (64), on the other hand, show utterances in which the verb is marked for a third person singular with the suffix –*s*, but the subject is not a third person singular subject but a plural one.

What is important as reflected in these examples is that none of the subject–verb disagreements shown involves a non-third person subject such as 'you' or 'we'. In other words, although subject–verb agreement may not be consistently marked in some speakers' speech, it is evident that these speakers are aware that subject–verb agreement involves only the third person subject. Subject–verb disagreement may simply be a result of the random morphological markings discussed in section 3.1 above.

3.5 Double subjects and zero subjects

As mentioned in the introduction to this chapter, it is frequently observed in the speech of Hong Kong English speakers that two noun phrases are present in the initial position of a sentence, the first being the topic, while the second is the grammatical subject. Although such a structure also exists in English, it is a marked construction with the topic commonly marked by complex prepositions such as 'As for . . .', 'Regarding . . .', and so on (McArthur 2002; Platt 1982). However, in Hong Kong English, due to the influence of the topic-prominence feature in Cantonese, the topic–comment [NP + clause] structure is very common (Green 1996). An example from McArthur (2002: 361) which has been used to illustrate this structure in Hong Kong English in the introductory section of this chapter is repeated below:

(66) Passengers who take the ferry service from Ma Liu Shui, <u>they</u> can enjoy a free ride from Tap Mun to Wong Shek.

(notice)

The feature of double subjects is indeed quite prevalent. A number of examples can be found in our data, as shown below in examples (67) to (75), in which the first item in the double subject is double-underlined, followed by the underlined second item:

(67) and then I remember that … um <u>my cousin</u> <u>they</u> actually took a few back home

{05-HE:03:09}

(68) and because <u>my sister</u> <u>she she</u> was living <u>she</u> is actually <u>she's</u> there now

{08-HE:00:12}

(69) yes I I … because <u>my mothers</u> er he he er <u>my mother</u> <u>she</u> has a er some friends who go to church regularly

{09-HE:00:13}

(70) <u>the the fish</u> <u>they</u> are not very sensitive to the shining hook

{09-HE:01:45}

(71) um yes both bo- <u>all of the children</u> <u>they</u> are still very young … I think I am one of the older

{09-HE:03:42}

(72) and then um … <u>every children</u> <u>they they</u> came with their parents and actually each tents um is a unit for a family

{09-HE:03:50}

(73) aha yes … but I I think in general <u>Hong Kong people</u> <u>they they</u> love to go to the … to see the nature because our city life is quite … quite high tech and … busy so

{09-HE:08:20}

(74) <u>Vancouver</u> <u>they</u> have high-rise buildings they have … relatively good food

{08-HE:01:07}

(75) and <u>my sisters and my mother</u> <u>we we</u> join the wild camp

{09-HE:00:27}

The nine examples above clearly indicate the widespread use of double subjects in utterances among Hong Kong English speakers. In each of the utterances extracted above, the speakers first identify the 'topic' of the sentence by using a noun phrase (double-underlined in the above examples), which, in fact, represents the topic of that utterance. Then, immediately following that noun phrase, a pronoun is used to start the 'comment' sentence and the pronoun is the grammatical subject of the sentence. For example, in extract (67), the pronoun *they* (referring to *my cousin*) is superfluous. Similarly, the repeated subjects of *she* (referring to *my sister*) in (68), *she* (referring to *my mother*) in (69), *they* (referring to *the fish*) in (70), *they* (referring to *all of the children*) in (71), *they* (referring to *every children*) in (72), and *they* (referring to *Hong Kong people*) in (73) are all indications of a topic–comment structure in these utterances.

Examples (74) and (75) are worthy of further discussion. These two examples provide evidence to verify that these utterances demonstrate a feature of double subjects rather than 'pronoun copying' (Platt 1982: 410). In extract (74), *Vancouver they have high-rise buildings they have . . . relatively good food*, the noun phrase indicating the topic is *Vancouver*, the name of a place, while the grammatical subject is the pronoun *they*, not *it*. Therefore, the pronoun is not a 'copy' of the first noun phrase in the utterance. Rather, the first noun phrase is the topic about the utterance. The grammatical subject pronoun refers to 'the people of Vancouver' so it is *they*. By the same token, in extract (75) *and my sisters and my mother we we join the wild camp*, the first noun phrase *my sisters and my mother* is the topic while the grammatical subject pronoun *we* does not refer to the topic; rather, its antecedent is 'my sisters, my mother and myself'. It is not a pronoun copy of the topic noun phrase. It is further evidence of the topic-prominence feature in Hong Kong English.

While some utterances contain double subjects, some have no grammatical subjects.

Since Cantonese allows subjectless sentences – and in the preceding sections, Hong Kong English has been shown to be influenced by Cantonese – it is logical to assume that subjectless sentences must be prevalent. However, this is not the case. In our data, subjectless sentences are rare – only three instances are found. Among these three, two omitted subjects occur in the relative clause. A number of scholars (Gisborne 2000; Newbrook 1988; Webster et al. 1987) have already identified subjectless relative clauses in Hong Kong English. Here are the examples from our data:

(76) that em cause <u>you've got one kind of melon is green</u> in colour
{05-HE:09:10}

(77) they er <u>they have something hang on</u> the trees and someone would
       sleep there

                                                              {05-HE:14:11}

(78) because er my father er it's it's that we had two of us so fath- <u>my father</u>
       <u>can only take care of two of us can not like go with many young kids</u>
       because it's too dangerous

                                                              {10-HE:03:45}

Strictly speaking, only in extract (78) is there a typical subjectless
sentence. The subject pronoun *he*, which refers to *my father*, in *can not
like go with many young kids* is omitted. In (76) and (77), it is the relative
pronouns in the two relative clauses that are omitted: *[Ø is green]* and *[Ø
hang on the trees]*. The subjects in the two main clauses are present: *[you've
got one kind of melon]* and *[they have something]*.

To summarise, it appears that the topic–comment discourse structure of Cantonese has led to the frequent occurrence of double subjects
in Hong Kong English. However, the typological difference between
Cantonese and English in permitting subjectless sentences does not
seem to result in the proliferation of subjectless sentences in Hong Kong
English.

3.6 Non-distinction between count and mass nouns

In section 3.4 above, it has been pointed out that Hong Kong English
does not consistently mark verbs for number. Similarly, in section 3.1,
it was also noted that some plural nouns are not marked for plurality.
In other words, the third person singular suffix -*s* as well as the plural
suffix -*s* is frequently omitted. In this section, the phenomenon involving nouns will be explored further.

On the surface, count nouns are nouns that can be enumerated.
Usually concrete objects are associated with countability, whereas mass
nouns often refer to abstract entities that are not countable. However,
the semantics of the nouns alone cannot determine countability; countability is more of a grammatical feature than a semantic one in Standard
English. For example, the noun *idea* is semantically abstract but it is
grammatically a count noun, while *bread* is semantically concrete but
grammatically a mass noun. In other words, the plural suffix can be
added to the count noun *idea* whereas it is not possible to add -*s* to
the mass noun *bread* because of English grammar, not because of the
meaning of these nouns. Chinese learners have problems with English
mass nouns such as *furniture, mail, bread* and *chalk* (Liu et al. 2006: 136)

because they tend to categorise count and mass nouns in terms of the semantics of the nouns: concrete individuated objects tend to be considered to be 'count' whereas abstract and intangible entities are considered to be 'mass'.

Similarly, this English grammatical feature poses problems for Cantonese speakers in general because in Cantonese, almost everything can be counted through a classifier system. Most mass nouns in English, such as *furniture, mail, bread* and *chalk*, can be counted in Cantonese through its classifier system and the distinction of count versus mass is not grammatically marked in Cantonese. This eventually shows up in Hong Kong English. In example (79) below (example (9) in section 3.1), it can be seen that the speaker uses the mass noun *trouble* first without the suffix -*s* and then uses *troubles* in the second instance within the same utterance:

> (79) um your brother never got into <u>trouble</u> . . . you were always the one getting in <u>troubles</u>
>
> {05-HE:12:04}

This example clearly reveals that Speaker 5 does not distinguish a count noun from a mass noun grammatically, and thus has chosen to use it sometimes as a mass noun, as in *got into trouble*, and sometimes as a count noun marked with the plural suffix -*s* as in *getting in troubles*.

Another example from our data suggests that the non-distinction between count and mass nouns has contributed a lot to the apparent morphological idiosyncrasies in Hong Kong English.

> (80) you have to get <u>all the equipments</u>
>
> {09-HE:04:53}

Extract (80) shows the use of a mass noun *equipment* with the plural suffix -*s*, as if it were a count noun. In the light of this count/mass non-distinction, some of the examples discussed in section 3.1 concerning the morphology of nouns in Hong Kong English should be re-analysed. Examples (1) and (2) are repeated below as (81) and (82). They are examples showing a singular count noun used in its bare form.

> (81) yes and you see . . . there there will be <u>giraffe</u>
>
> {09-MT:03:30}

> (82) but the fact is um so people is always peoples are always afraid of <u>mosquito</u> some insects
>
> {09-HE:04:32}

In the examples above, the two count nouns *mosquito* and *giraffe* occur in their singular form without an article when they are used for generic reference. This usage is treating these two count nouns like mass nouns because it is the abstract concept that has been referred to. It appears that the semantics of these nouns has priority in determining the grammar.

The impact of the count/mass non-distinction has led to another grammatical feature concerning the use of the articles. The variable use of articles, a grammatical category which is absent in Cantonese, is a common feature among Hong Kong English speakers. Platt (1982: 410) has provided some examples to show the under-use of indefinite articles and the over-use of definite articles. These examples are quoted below:

(83) say you're doing receptionist job

(84) you can see de China right across

(85) I can take the snake but I can't take the dog meat

He has especially pointed out that the definite article is used for generic reference. Although this is not very frequent in our data, one example can illustrate the same feature:

(86) so we can feed it with <u>the banana</u>

{10-HE:02:48}

In this example, the noun phrase *the banana* does not actually refer to one particular banana but to bananas in general.

3.7 Word order: modifiers immediately precede heads

In noun phrases, another common feature which is typical of Hong Kong English is the tendency to stack nouns together, either by forming 'compound nouns', as in examples (87), (88) and (89), or by using the possessive constructions, as in (90) and (91).

(87) so that's why I was very excited but um ... it it takes so much time to arrive to the camp camp site um and then I think it takes er ... it tooks er more than <u>an hour travel</u> by bus

{09-HE:00:46}

(88) so we walk another two hours and then <u>one hour bus</u> and ... came back to the city

{09-HE:02:18}

(89) but they are <u>very small scale one</u> for children

{10-HE:01:34}

(90) yes um but the funny thing is there lots of um um <u>cows' faeces</u>

{09-HE:01:11}

(91) so if you don't keep yourself in the air con room you m- you will possibly be disturbed by the <u>traffic's noise</u>

{09-HE:08:58}

The five noun phrases in the examples above can be analysed in the
following way:

(87′) [*an hour travel*] ➔ [[*an hour*] *travel*]

(88′) [*one hour bus*] ➔ [[*one hour*] *bus*]

(89′) [*very small scale one*] ➔ [[*very small scale*] *one*]

(90′) [*cows' faeces*] ➔ [[*cows'*] *faeces*]

(91′) [*traffic's noise*] ➔ [[*traffic's*] *noise*]

It can be seen that all the noun phrases analysed above consist of a head
noun modified by another noun phrase which precedes it. This head-
final characteristic of noun phrases in Hong Kong English is probably
influenced by Cantonese, which tends to be head-final, too.

The head-final phrase structure is also found in the placement of
adverbs by Hong Kong English speakers (A. Chan 2004a). The following example from A. Chan (2004a: 63) illustrates this point:

(92) he very like dancing

In Standard English, the intensifier *very* is usually used together with
much to form an adverb phrase and the adverb phrase is placed after the
verb, but here the adverb *very* is placed immediately before the verb to
modify it. A similar example of this type is found in our data, shown in
example (93) below:

(93) I so later I <u>more enjoy</u> doing this rather than going er a wild camp but
I I do do a lot of hiking

{09-HE:07:58}

In example (93), the intensifier *more* is used immediately before the
verb rather than after the verb phrase. If we compare [. . . *[more] enjoy*

doing this] with [. . . *enjoy doing this [more]*], it is evident that in Hong Kong English, the modifier [*more*] occurs before the head verb [*enjoy*], whereas this is not the case in Standard English. It has been shown that Hong Kong English prefers the [modifier–head] structure; therefore, it is not difficult to understand why a noun phrase involving the modifier *quite* tends to have a structure like the following, different from Standard English:

(94) well I got <u>a quite interesting</u> childhood

{05-HE:00:00}

In this structure, the Standard English version is [*quite an interesting childhood*]. The adverb *quite* which is assumed to modify an adjective does not occur immediately before the head adjective *interesting*. Instead, it occurs before the indefinite article *a*, making *quite* appear to be a pre-determiner. However, it is very common in Hong Kong English that the normal structure of a noun phrase where the modifier *quite* occurs immediately before the head adjective is used:

Hong Kong English: [article [adverb + head adjective] noun]
[*a quite interesting childhood*]
Standard English: [pre-determiner [article [adjective] noun]]
[*quite an interesting childhood*]

This is another manifestation of the head-final feature in which the modifier immediately precedes the head it modifies.

3.8 Prepositions and transitivity

There are a number of examples in our data where the redundant use of a preposition in Hong Kong English is observed.

(95) um yeah to the yeah that's right and then you can see um so just just pass <u>through </u>the erm safari truck

{05-MT:02:47}

(96) um so if you see a springboks pass <u>through</u> it and then go north and then

{09-MT:01:12}

(97) yeah please pass <u>through</u> it

{10-MT:00:04}

(98) and so after you pass <u>through</u> the highest view point

{10-MT:01:13}

(99) please pass <u>through</u> them

{10-MT:03:42}

(100) so you have to um . . . um . . . you have to face <u>to</u> the south

{05-MT:00:05}

Extracts (95) to (99) involve the verb *pass* followed by the preposition *through*, and (100) involves the verb *face* followed by the preposition *to*. In each case, the preposition is redundant. The fact that the examples came from three of the five speakers in our data indicates how prevalent this structure is. What is in focus appears to be a redundant preposition, but in fact, this is an issue of transitivity. The redundant preposition is used because the verbs *pass* and *face* are treated as an intransitive verb and the noun phrase immediately following them is linked by a preposition. A. Chan (2004a: 64–5) has pointed out that Hong Kong English students are confused about the transitivity of some English verbs. They regard some intransitive verbs as transitive, so a noun phrase is used immediately after the verb as if it were the direct object. Examples (101) and (102) below are taken from A. Chan (2004a: 65), and (103) is from Bolton and Nelson (2002: 261). These three examples resemble (104), which is found in our data.

(101) we must care the old people

(102) he very like listening music

(103) You care only Cheng Siu Chau

(104) ok so if you arrive the safari truck you go um a bit er . . . south west

{09-MT:01:49}

The same speaker, interestingly, has used *arrive* with a prepositional phrase, treating *arrive* as an intransitive verb in another context:

(105) I think before you you arrive <u>to</u> the mountain you will see the springboks

{09-MT:01:06}

Although there are not many examples found in our data, we have, in this section, shown that the omission or the inappropriate use of prepositions found in Hong Kong English is related to transitivity.

3.9 Conversion of grammatical categories

One more grammatical feature found in our database is the ease in grammatical category conversion, an influence from Cantonese. Matthews and Yip (1994: 55) have noted the difference between English and Cantonese in category conversion:

> Both English and Cantonese allow limited conversion of one part of speech to another. However, the two languages differ with respect to the range of possibilities of conversion. For example, while any verb in Cantonese can appear in subject and object positions without change in form, verbs in English generally take on affixes if they are to appear in these positions: *criticise* → *criticism; swim* → *swimming; destroy* → *destruction.*

In the examples below, Hong Kong English speakers demonstrate the use of prepositions as verbs: *along* in extract (106) and *towards* in (107); the use of a preposition as an adverb: *away* in (108); the use of a verb as an adjective: *demand* in (109); and the use of an adjective as a noun: *distant* in (110).[4]

(106) just <u>alonged</u> it   (Prep → V)

                                            {05-MT:06:21}

(107) yeah so um er just walk towards the great lake um area just <u>towards</u> that just go straight   (Prep → V)

                                            {05-MT:06:01}

(108) so even you go very <u>away</u> from the cities you still find a lot of people   (Prep → Adv)

                                            {09-HE:06:07}

(109) yeah so it's less physically <u>demand</u> and after like six hours' walk I can go back to my home and have   (V → Adj)

                                            {09-HE:08:08}

(110) there's still a- <u>distant</u>   (Adj → N)

                                            {05-MT:04:37}

The use of the preposition *along* as a verb in (106) is the most interesting. The speaker even adds the past tense suffix to the preposition *along*, clearly treating it as a verb. This tendency of category conversion is another typical feature of Hong Kong English.

3.10 Summary

The spoken data that have been analysed in this chapter demonstrate a number of morphological and grammatical features in Hong Kong English. In terms of morphological markings, it is evident that Hong Kong English speakers do not consistently use the plural suffix to mark plural nouns, or use -*s* to mark third person singular verbs. Similarly, the -*ed* suffix is not always found in the regular past tense or the past participle of verbs. On the other hand, some morphological features are doubly marked. This may be attributed to the influence from Cantonese, a language which has very little morphology. Another factor which may contribute to the morphological features in Hong Kong English is the irregular morphology of English itself.

The grammatical features found in Hong Kong English involve all grammatical categories. As is the case with phonology, although most features are clearly a result of the interaction between English and Cantonese, not all of the features in Hong Kong English can be attributed to this factor alone.

At the sentential level, double subjects are quite common. And while subject omission can be found, it is not very frequent. With regard to verbs, tense use seems to be confined to only three: the present, the past and the future; tense switching is very frequent; subject–verb disagreement is found but is clearly related to morphology. In terms of nouns, count/mass noun non-distinction may be an underlying factor for the non-marking of plural nouns. The head-final phrase structure is especially evident in noun phrases.

The other two features – preposition use showing transitivity differences and category conversion – are not very prominent in our data. Although they seem minor, these have not been extensively studied before. We definitely need to conduct more systematic investigation before any conclusive description can be provided.

Having provided a comprehensive view of the morphological and grammatical features of Hong Kong English, we will now turn to discourse and lexis in the next chapter.

Notes

1. For a detailed description of the differences between English and Chinese with reference to topic-prominence and subject-prominence, see Yip (1995: 73–95).

2. This is further complicated by the phonological feature of some Hong Kong English speakers who tend to insert an extra [s] in word-final position, as discussed in section 2.4 in this volume.

3. In English morphology, verbs are only inflected for two tenses: past and present. English verbs are not inflected for the future tense and thus some syntacticians argue that there are in fact only two tenses in English. For simplicity of presentation in this book, we will include future as one of the tenses used by Hong Kong English speakers.

4. List of abbreviations for the grammatical categories given in the examples: Adj = Adjective, Adv = Adverb, N = noun, Prep = preposition, V = verb.

4 Discourse and lexis

Discourse features in Hong Kong English have not received much attention; for example, Bolton (2002a) includes chapters which deal with phonology (Hung 2000, reprinted in Bolton 2002a), grammar (Gisborne 2000, reprinted in Bolton 2002a) and lexis (Benson 2000, reprinted in Bolton 2002a), but there is no chapter on discourse. Nor is there much discussion in Bolton (2003), Kachru (2005) or Kachru and Nelson (2006), the latter two works looking at the broader context of Asian Englishes. One recent attempt to fill this gap is Wong (2007), which is an analysis of the forms and functions of question tags in the International Corpus of English, Hong Kong component (ICE-HK). Added to this are a number of corpus-based studies which compare the use of English discourse features between Hong Kong speakers and native speakers (Cheng and Warren 2001a, 2001b; Fung and Carter 2007b), but these studies do not presume a distinctive variety of Hong Kong English, generally referring to Hong Kong speakers as non-native speakers (NNS) or students, and their findings are not always consistent with our data. It may be more useful, therefore, to look at the discourse features which Deterding (2007) discusses in relation to Singapore English, as these may be relevant to Hong Kong English, given common substrate influence from Cantonese.

Compared with discourse, there has been more discussion of vocabulary in Hong Kong English; see for example Benson (2000), Bolton (2003), Carless (1995), Chow (2001), Cummings (2007) and Taylor (1989). These studies draw their data from certain genres or kinds of discourse. For example, much attention has been paid to Hong Kong English vocabulary in newspapers (Taylor 1989; Carless 1995), and many vocabulary items identified in newspapers are specifically related to political discourse, which is the topic of corpus study in Chow (2001). Bolton (2003) includes a comprehensive list of Hong Kong English vocabulary items as an appendix (Bolton 2003: 288–97, Appendix 5). Although most recently Cummings (2007) has compiled a glossary in which he identified examples of Hong Kong English vocabulary in all kinds of written discourse or print media, including newspaper, magazines, comic strips, novels and weblogs, not much is known about the state of Hong Kong vocabulary in other kinds of genres or discourse, especially in everyday spoken discourse.

Benson (2002) proposes some criteria for the existence or autonomy of Hong Kong English vocabulary items. For instance, these lexical items are only properly understood in the context of Hong Kong (social, cultural, historical, economic and so on) and in relation to other Hong Kong vocabulary items. One particularly insightful example which Benson (2002: 167) gives is *the mainland* or *mainland China*, which is understood as meaning China without including Hong Kong, Macau or Taiwan, regions that were or are politically separate from The People's Republic of China (PRC). The term is still used in Hong Kong very productively, as indicated by the currency of such expressions as *mainlanders, mainland people, mainland students, mainland scholars, mainland officials, mainland tourists* and so on, even though Hong Kong has been a Special Administrative Region (SAR) of the PRC since 1997. In other words, the opposition between *Hong Kong* and *the mainland* persists, even though Hong Kong is, strictly speaking, part of China. Taking a Hong Kong perspective, even coastal areas of China such as Fujian (福建) or Shandong (山東) would be conceived as the part of 'the mainland'.

As observed in Bolton (2003), in spite of the creativity and autonomy of Hong Kong English vocabulary, expressions are formed by many regular word-formation processes such as *borrowing, loan translation, acronym* or *compounding* which apply to other emergent or New Englishes (for example, Singapore English; see Deterding 2007) and indeed all natural languages around the world. In this chapter we detail common Hong Kong English expressions classified according to different word-formation processes such as these. Many of these entries are also listed in Bolton (2003: 288–98, Appendix 5), Cummings (2007) and other works on Hong Kong English vocabulary.

4.1 Discourse markers

Discourse markers (or DMs), such as *well* in English, are those words or expressions which signal speaker attitude or relations between stretches of discourse without much contribution to the propositional meaning of a sentence. Fung and Carter (2007b) discuss the use of English DMs in a corpus of Hong Kong students' speech with reference to another corpus of British speakers, the Cambridge and Nottingham Corpus of Discourse in English (CANCODE). The Hong Kong speakers were found to produce a limited range of discourse markers in comparison with the British speakers. Out of twenty-three DMs, twelve discourse markers found in CANCODE were used much less frequently in the Hong Kong corpus, such as *yeah*, *right*, *you know* and *well*, in particular 'interpersonal' DMs which indicate shared knowledge (for example, *you know*) or speaker attitude (for example, *well*, which indicates reservation towards a topic). On the other hand, four DMs are much more frequent in the Hong Kong corpus: *I think*, *yes*, *but* and *because*. The Hong Kong students in Fung and Carter's study used *but* and *because* primarily as connectors which signal relationships between utterances. The use of *I think*, which indicates politeness or hedging, is considered 'routinised' or 'fossilised' (Fung and Carter 2007b: 431). As for *yes*, Fung and Carter (2007b: 431–3) suggest that its frequency in the Hong Kong corpus may be the result of Hong Kong speakers using the DM where British speakers would have used *yeah*.

The rarity of interpersonal DMs does not apply to our data. For instance, Speaker 1 uses *you know* frequently, but that is admittedly less common in the data of our other four speakers. All five speakers in our data produce some instances of *yeah*, either as responses to the interviewer's questions or as a backchannel to him. These differences may be due to the fact that our speakers are adults who are more experienced in getting along with native speakers of English in Britain and hence they have developed a higher pragmatic competence in using the interpersonal DMs.

The DMs commonly used in Fung and Carter's student corpus (2007b) do not always correspond with the ones which are high-frequency in our data either. For example, the students use *I think* frequently in Fung and Carter's (2007b) corpus, but our data show that only Speaker 5 and Speaker 9 produce many instances of *I think*. Other speakers seldom use the expression, or, in the case of Speaker 8, never use it, as shown in Table 4.1.

Contrary to Fung and Carter's data, all of the speakers in our data used some instances of *actually*, although there are in fact not many more tokens (see Table 4.2).

In Fung and Carter's (2007b) corpus, however, the students produced fewer instances of *actually* than the native speakers did. Our data appear to be more compatible with Cheng and Warren (2001b), who found many more tokens of *actually* produced by Hong Kong speakers. This, along with the function of *actually* in Hong Kong English, is discussed in the next section.

Table 4.1 Occurrences of *I think* in the data of Hong Kong speakers (total = 24)

	Speaker 1	Speaker 5	Speaker 8	Speaker 9	Speaker 10
Happy event	1	10	0	10	3
Map task	0	0	0	0	0
Total	1	10	0	10	3

Table 4.2 Occurrences of *actually* in the data of Hong Kong speakers (total = 31)

	Speaker 1	Speaker 5	Speaker 8	Speaker 9	Speaker 10
Happy event	2	10	4	5	1
Map task	5	2	0	1	1
Total	7	12	4	6	2

4.2 *Actually* in spoken discourse

In Cheng and Warren's (2001b) study, which uses a corpus of English conversation between Hong Kong speakers and non-Hong Kong speakers (mostly native speakers of English), Hong Kong speakers produce almost three times more tokens of *actually* than the non-Hong Kong speakers. It was concluded that the high frequency of *actually* is 'a distinguishing feature of Hong Kong English' (Cheng and Warren 2001b: 276).

Among the pragmatic functions of *actually* that Cheng and Warren (2001b) consider, Hong Kong speakers most often use *actually* to 'indicate a situation exists or happened', and quite often the word is also used to 'emphasise something unexpected is true or correct', to 'mitigate correction, rephrasing or contradiction' or to 'introduce a new topic or sub-topic' (Cheng and Warren 2001b: 269). Cheng and Warren (2001b: 270) explain the dominance of these functions tentatively in terms of Chinese 'face', which is supposed to have a heavy influence on Hong Kong speakers, the idea being that these speakers are anxious to seek recognition of their statements or ideas rather than being genuinely liked by others. Native speakers of English may well fulfil these functions by using DMs other than *actually*, such as *really* or *well*, which are used much less frequently by Hong Kong speakers (Cheng and Warren 2001b: 276). This also helps to explain the high frequency of *actually* in the speech of Hong Kong speakers. Another difference between Hong Kong speakers and non-Hong Kong speakers is that the former group

Table 4.3 Occurrences of *actually* in different positions in the data of Hong Kong speakers (total = 31)

Clause-initial position	Clause-medial position	Clause-final position	Single-word utterance
12 (38.71%)	16 (51.61%)	2 (6.45%)	1 (3.23%)

rarely uses *actually* for interpersonal functions such as conveying solidarity, friendliness or intimacy (Cheng and Warren 2001b: 258) or in sentence-final position (Cheng and Warren 2001b: 274).

Our data generally conform to Cheng and Warren's findings. The word *actually* is found across all five speakers, indicating that it is indeed a common discourse feature amongst Hong Kong speakers. Most occurrences of *actually* are in either clause-initial or clause-medial positions. Only a few tokens appear in clause-final position, all of which are produced by Speaker 2, suggesting that this position is not common for *actually* in Hong Kong English (see Table 4.3).

The following are some examples in our data which fit into the pragmatic functions of *actually* as laid out in Cheng and Warren (2001b).

(1) *Indicate a situation indeed exists*:
Vancouver is <u>actually</u> quite different from Edmonton.
{08-HE:01:02}

(2) *Mitigate correction*. The speaker had said that her sister <u>*was* *living*</u> in Edmonton but she corrected the statement to *she's there now*.
because my sister she she was living she is <u>actually</u> she's there now she's living in Edmonton a little town in Canada
{08-HE:00:12}

(3) *Introduce a new topic or subtopic*. The speaker had been talking about her weekend activities with parents.
05: yeah . . . but I think it's very interesting maybe because of these kind of thing I was quite childish in a way
Int: mhm
05: cause erm like I <u>actually</u> didn't understand a lot of things that my classmate erm talk about
{05-HE:06:36}

(4) *Act as a filler*. The speaker seemed to be figuring out what he wanted to say, as suggested by the repetition of *I wanna* and another filler *you know*.
Int: so you enjoyed playing with Legos at that time

01:     yeah last week I went to London I <u>actually</u> I wanna I wanna you
        know play that with the kids you know around me

{01-HE:04:53}

(5) *Introduce or mitigate a point of view.* The speaker had been saying that
    many people were noisy in rural areas where they went camping.
    so <u>actually</u> we just bring the the city life to the . . . to to the rural area
    ((laugh)) aha

{09-HE:06:50}

(6) *Imply a sense of solidarity, friendliness or intimacy.* The speaker was talking
    about some fish that her cousins brought home and that grew horribly
    fast. The single-word *actually* looks like a response to the interviewer's
    backchanelling *mhm.*
    05:     ((laughs)) but it's so horrible it . . . they they really didn't look
            like fish at all . . . it's very strange I don't know what they they
            are
    Int: mhm
    05:     <u>actually</u>

{05-HE:04:36}

There are also instances that cannot be clearly classified into a category in Cheng and Warren's (2001b) taxonomy.

(7) yes I stayed in Hong Kong <u>actually</u> for my life before I came here
{08-HE:04:36}

In example (7) above, the speaker may be using *actually* to introduce
a new subtopic (*for my life*) or to indicate that something is indeed the
case (that is, *It is true that I stayed in Hong Kong for my life*). A more fitting
description, however, seems to be that *actually* is used to introduce more
specific or precise information to the current topic, an *elaborative* function that can be served by other discourse markers such as *in fact, I mean*
or *more precisely.* Two more examples in which *actually* serves a similar
elaborative function are given below. It is possible that *actually* in extract
(8) may act as a filler, or to mitigate rephrasing.

(8) and then um . . . every children they they came with their parents and
    <u>actually</u> each tents um is a unit for a family

{09-HE:03:50}

(9) so at that time I went there and . . . <u>actually</u> I went there with my
    brother and my father

{10-HE:00:33}

Instances of a*ctually* in its elaborative function can be found in the map task data, too. In the examples below, the speakers are guiding the interviewer around the map towards the destination.

(10) yeah so there's <u>actually</u> a path between those two

{01-MT:01:53}

(11) I see <u>actually</u> the gold mine is er ... at the midway of banana tree and rock fill

{09-MT:03:05}

It may well be the case that Hong Kong speakers seldom use *actually* to convey a sense of solidarity or involvement (Cheng and Warren 2001b), an exception being example (6) above. None the less, the Hong Kong speakers did use the word for some interpersonal functions. In the map task, the speakers give instructions to the interviewer, and they sometimes use *actually* as a face-saving act (Brown and Levinson 1987) to mitigate or soften the weight of imposition of the instructions.

(12) and you <u>actually</u> go south

{01-MT:00:12}

(13) can I <u>actually</u> um estimate you know the time frame and to give you directions

{01-MT:04:49}

(14) ah <u>actually</u> if you keep walking straight you can see the springboks

{10-MT:00:13}

4.3 *Because* and *so* in spoken discourse

Another DM frequently used in Fung and Carter's (2007b) corpus is *because*. Although all the speakers in our corpus did produce a fair number of tokens of *because*, they used *so* even more frequently. Table 4.4 shows the number of tokens of *because* or *cos*/*'cause* produced by our speakers, and Table 4.5 shows the number of tokens of *so* in our data.

The higher frequency of *so* over *because* is probably not a distinctive feature of Hong Kong English as this is expected from the versatility of *so* in discourse; *because* is primarily a connector used to introduce a CAUSE clause, whereas *so* is not only a connector (introducing a RESULT clause) but also a device to indicate turn-taking; that is, the listener may pick up a turn by starting with *so* (Schiffrin 1987). There is perhaps one feature in our data which is characteristic of Hong Kong English; that is,

Table 4.4 Occurrences of *because* or *cos*/*'cause* in the data of Hong Kong speakers (total = 57)

	Speaker 1	Speaker 5	Speaker 8	Speaker 9	Speaker 10
Happy event	11	17[a]	12	11	4
Map task	0	0	1	0	1
Total	11	17	13	11	5

[a] including one reformulation

Table 4.5 Occurrences of *so* in the data of Hong Kong speakers (total = 111)

	Speaker 1	Speaker 5	Speaker 8	Speaker 9	Speaker 10
Happy event	14[a]	11[b]	4	25[d]	10
Map task	9	19[c]	0	14[e]	5
Total	23	30	4	39	15

[a] including three repetitions or reformulations
[b] including one reformulation
[c] including three repetitions or reformulations
[d] including one reformulation
[e] including two repetitions or reformulations

the use of *because*/*cos* and *so* consecutively to mark a CAUSE clause and an immediately following RESULT clause in a complex sentence. All five speakers in our data use some instances of this pattern.

(15) because kids love fries and fried pan-fried stuff and so yeah my dad would take us there

{01-HE:02:00}

(16) because their mother didn't like them [that is, *some fish*] a lot . . . so they let them go back to the river

{05-HE:04:54}

(17) because . . . she said that she does not have any time to cook . . . so erm usually erm the cook I was the cook

{08-HE:03:58}

(18) because Hong Kong is small or we have too many people . . . so even you go very away from the cities you still find a lot of people

{09-HE:06:04}

(19) because is some kind of domestic elephant . . . it's not wild . . . so it's very well behaved

{10-HE:03:34}

In British English, particularly in written discourse, only one connector is necessary, either *because* or *so*, but in spoken discourse native speakers may sometimes use both connectors, producing sentences which look like examples (15) to (19) (Schiffrin 1987: 193). Furthermore, there is flexibility as to the order of the CAUSE clause and the RESULT clause; that is, both CAUSE–RESULT (that is, '*Because X, Y*' or '*X, so Y*') and RESULT–CAUSE ('*Y, because X*') are permissible orders. In Hong Kong English, the use of *because–so* is perhaps more frequent owing to influence from Cantonese, in which a fixed order of CAUSE–RESULT clauses is marked by two DMs such as *jan1-wai6*/因爲 *(because)* and *so2-ji5*/所以 *(so)*. The CAUSE–RESULT order instantiates an *inductive* pattern of reasoning preferred in Asian cultures over a *deductive* pattern of reasoning (RESULT–CAUSE; see Scollon 1993; Scollon and Scollon 2000).

4.4 Topic–comment sentences

Topic–comment sentences such as extract (20) appear to be common not only in Hong Kong English but also in Singapore English (Deterding 2007: 62–3), as well as in other varieties in the Outer and Expanding Circles (Kachru and Nelson 2006: 47; see also section 6.4 in this volume).

(20) <u>the the fish</u>   <u>they</u> are not very sensitive to the shining hook
      TOPIC   COMMENT

                                                  {09-HE:01:45}

   Topic–comment sentences straddle syntax and discourse, and, as such, we refer to them under section 3.5 as 'double subjects', as well as in this chapter. As a recap, grammatically speaking, topic–comment structures apparently have two subjects, that is, the topic (for example, *the fish* in extract (20)) and the subject of the comment clause (for example, *they* in (20)). In Chapter 3, it is mentioned that the production of these topic–comment sentences is presumably due to the influence of Cantonese, in which these structures are extremely common (Cantonese is said to be *topic-prominent*). In section 3.5, a number of topic–comment sentences in our Hong Kong English data are given as examples. It is further pointed out that the subject in the comment clause is not necessarily a pronoun referring to the topic; for example, *they* in example (21) does not exactly refer to *Vancouver* but rather *people in Vancouver*.

(21) <u>Vancouver</u> they have high-rise buildings they have . . . relatively
               good food
     TOPIC   COMMENT

{08-HE:01:07}

In discourse analysis, topic encodes an entity which is given or shared information among speakers, whereas comment provides some new or relevant information about the topic. In other words, topic–comment sentences are one way of organising information in a sentence. In his description of Singapore English, Deterding (2007) treats topic–comment sentences as both a grammatical feature and a discourse feature.

It is not surprising to find topic–comment sentences in Singapore English, which is also under the influence of Cantonese (and actually, Deterding (2007: 62) suggests that topic-prominence in Singapore English may be due to the influence of Malay as well). There is, however, some difference between Deterding's Singapore English data and our Hong Kong English data. In our data, topic is mostly related to the subject of the comment clause in some way (for example, extracts (20) and (21)). The following example is an exception in our data; in this example, the topic (that is, *everything he did*) corresponds to the object of the comment clause which is empty (that is, the object of *follow*).

(22) everything he did I would follow . . . whatever
     TOPIC   COMMENT

{05-HE:11:58}

Contrastively, Singapore English shows a wider range of topics which may correspond to subjects of the comment clause (for example, extract (23)) or objects of the comment clause (for example, (24)), or that may be some expression not related to any grammatical function in the comment clause (for example, (25)) (Deterding 2007).

(23) basically my sisters, they will buy magazines like Her World
     TOPIC   COMMENT

(Deterding 2007: 64)

(24) so the process I need to put down for different operators
     TOPIC   COMMENT

(Deterding 2007: 63)

(25) colleagues-wise, I enjoy teaching in ern Princess E
     TOPIC   COMMENT

(Deterding 2007: 63)

4.5 Utterance-final particles

Another distinctive feature of Singapore English is the use of utterance-final particles, which originate from various Chinese dialects (or languages) such as Cantonese or Hokkien (that is, Fujianese) (Deterding 2007). The following is an example.

> (26) They do have shopping area <u>lah</u>
>
> (Deterding 2007: 70)

Interestingly, this feature seems to be rare in spoken Hong Kong English, which is similarly under the influence of Chinese or Cantonese. None the less, these utterance-final particles are much more widespread after English sentences in electronic communication (for example, electronic mail, ICQ,[1] MSN and, more recently, social networking websites such as Facebook) involving Hong Kong speakers of English (Chan 1999; Fung and Carter 2007a; Ho 2006; Lee 2007). These utterance-final particles are often represented in English spelling as *la, lor, ah, ar, tim, wor* and so on. They are a discourse feature in Hong Kong English which is specific to the medium of internet communication. Here are some examples from the literature:

> (27) talk to you later <u>lar</u>
>
> (Ho 2006: 443)

> (28) The ocamp [*orientation camp*] is ok <u>la</u>
>
> (Lee 2007: 198)

> (29) I didn't get enough sleep the night before <u>lor</u>
>
> (Fung and Carter 2007a: 44)

4.6 Question tags in spoken discourse

A common feature in spoken discourse, a tag question consists of a statement, or an 'anchor', and a 'question tag' (Huddleston and Pullum 2002). In British English, a question tag contrasts with the anchor in terms of polarity, but the modal or auxiliary verb in the question tag agrees with that in the anchor. The auxiliary verb *do* is used if there is no modal or auxiliary verb in the anchor; for example:

> (30) You like butter,   don't you? (polarity: positive–negative)
>   ANCHOR   QUESTION TAG

Question tags perform a range of different pragmatic functions; for instance, the 'informatory' function, whereby the speaker seeks information from the listener, and the 'confirmatory' function, whereby the speaker is unsure of the anchor statement and seeks confirmation from the listener. Question tags may also signal the speaker's belief in or conviction of the proposition (as expressed in the anchor) rather than seeking information or confirmation, the so-called 'attitudinal' function (Tottie and Hoffman 2006). Tottie and Hoffmann (2006) found a number of differences between British English and American English in the form and function of tag questions. Question tags may well be an area where varieties of English show systematic variation.

Comparing a corpus of conversational English produced by Hong Kong speakers with another one produced by native speakers of English, Cheng and Warren (2001a) found that Hong Kong speakers use many fewer question tags than do the British speakers. Among the tags in the Hong Kong corpus, the two forms *is it* and *isn't it* appear frequently, and in many instances they do not agree with the modal or auxiliary verb in the anchor. Most data take the form of positive–negative constructions, which Cheng and Warren (2001a) attribute to transfer from Cantonese, the mother tongue of the Hong Kong speakers in the study. The most common pragmatic function of the tags used by the Hong Kong speakers is the confirmatory function, where speakers seek approval of the listener to the anchor. British speakers, on the other hand, most often use the tags to seek information, that is, the informatory function, and to emphasise the statement they have just expressed, that is, the attitudinal function. The high frequency of confirmatory tags used by Hong Kong speakers may well reflect an attempt to couch politeness and co-operation with listeners. The overall rarity of question tags in Hong Kong speakers' data may be attributed to various factors: for instance, they may use other forms to fulfil the informatory function, such as the word tag *right*. It may be argued that they lack socio-pragmatic competence in using question tags. Alternatively, it is possible that they do not often produce question tags because of the influence of Cantonese, which does not make use of question tags.

In a more recent study, Wong (2007) examined a much larger sample, numbering 197 instances of question tags drawn from the corpus ICE-HK. In this dataset, alongside the common positive–negative constructions, there was a high percentage of positive–positive constructions which deviated from British or American English. As for the form of the question tag, the tag *is it* accounted for nearly 40 per cent of the total number of question tags. What's more, in many of these instances, *be* was simply not used in the anchor. The use of *is it* as a universal tag is

apparently a distinctive characteristic of Hong Kong English not paral-
leled in other new varieties of English, in which *isn't it* is more common.
In addition, many other auxiliary or modal verbs in the tag do not match
with those in the anchor; for instance, *Can they overlap anyway, don't they*,
another pattern which is different from British English. In Wong's
(2007) data, most question tags serve either a confirmatory function or
an attitudinal function.

Consistent with the findings of Cheng and Warren (2001a), question
tags are rare in our data. Interestingly, there are a few instances of question tags used by the interviewer. He is not a native speaker of English
(see section 1.5 in Chapter 1), and yet his question tags largely conform
to the norms of British English.

> (31) it's not very comfortable is it
>   (polarity: negative–positive, function: confirmatory)
>   {Interviewer with 09-HE:04:57}

4.7 Written discourse

There has been very little research on written discourse in Hong Kong
English. Here, we report on two studies which look at this area, and
show that, in written discourse, where many interpersonal DMs (for
example, *well, sort of* etc.) are rare, differences between Hong Kong
speakers and native speakers are not obvious.

Bolton et al. (2002) investigate the use of English connectors in
ICE-HK and the British component of the same corpus (ICE-GB), and
conclude that Hong Kong speakers and British speakers use a similar
range of connectors with comparable frequency. The informants of the
datasets are students, and, as expected, both groups use a limited range
of connectors in comparison with professional academics (Bolton et al.
2002: 180).

Looking at a corpus of political commentary written by mostly Hong
Kong Chinese authors, Berry (1999/2000) found that the first person
plural pronoun (mostly *we*, but also *our* and *us*) is used predominantly
for *generic* reference whereby the pronoun stands for the Hong Kong
community. In many cases, these instances of the first person plural
pronoun are anaphoric to other lexical expressions, such as *the community, Hong Kong, Hong Kong people, local people* and *the territory* (Berry
1999/2000: 18–19). However, it remains to be seen whether the generic
use of pronouns extends to texts other than the newspaper genre in
Hong Kong English.

Clearly, further research is needed in the area of written discourse in Hong Kong English. This is not due to a lack of material, as a lot of communication takes place in written form in the workplace, as well as in newspapers and academic settings. However, we observe that this is an area which has not received much attention in other, similar varieties of English either. For example, Deterding (2007) does not have much to say on this matter concerning Singapore English. We conclude that it is possible that Hong Kong English (and possibly Singapore English) is not so very different from varieties such as British or American English in this regard.

We now move on to discuss aspects of lexis in Hong Kong English. We first discuss different word-formation processes in the vocabulary of Hong Kong English, followed by some examples attested in electronic communication and in our data.

4.8 Lexis

The following description of word-formation processes largely follows Bauer (1983), Bolton (2003) and Yule (2003). These include borrowing, coinage, compounding and affixation. As noted so often in linguistic analysis, it may be difficult to classify an example unambiguously as belonging to a certain word-formation process or category, as a word may undergo multiple processes (Yule 2003).

Since our data do not cover a wide range of vocabulary, a large portion of the data on which the following analysis is based come from Chan and Kwok (1985), Benson (2002), and Bolton (2003).

4.9 Borrowing

Borrowings, or loanwords, originate from pre-existing words in another language. Borrowing is a common process of forming new words, especially in times of language and culture contact. Bolton (2003: 288–97) collated a list of the vocabulary items of Hong Kong English, 51 per cent of which are loanwords (Bolton 2003: 214). Many of them have been borrowed from Chinese (Mandarin) or Cantonese. They usually reflect cultural practices or objects which are exclusively associated with Chinese culture, and which are difficult to codify in English, for example, *dim-sum* and *feng shui*. The loanword *dim-sum*, according to Chan and Kwok (1985: 233), means 'tidbits eaten at a Cantonese repast taken either in the early morning or at lunch time known as yamcha or "drinking tea"'. *Fung shui* refers to 'a kind of geomancy for . . . determining sites for houses and graves' (Chan and Kwok 1985: 235).

These are examples where transliteration is employed when lexical items are borrowed from the source language: *fung* means 'wind' and *shui* means 'water' in Cantonese.

While lexical items borrowed through phonetic transliteration assume a pronunciation near that of words in the source language, it is well known that they often undergo phonological integration into the borrowing language (Grosjean 1982; Romaine 1995). Borrowings from Cantonese to English preserve the phonetic shape of their source expressions, and hence Chan and Kwok (1985) call them 'phonetic loans'; none the less, phonological adaptation does take place. For instance, the velar plosive at the beginning of *gung1-fu1*[2] ('martial arts' in Cantonese) is voiceless and unaspirated in Cantonese ([k]), but pronounced as an aspirated stop [kʰ] in *kung-fu* (Hong Kong English). The consonant at the start of the second syllable of *yum-cha* (drink tea) is pronounced as a palato-alveolar affricate [tʃ] in English, but in Cantonese it is actually pronounced as a dental affricate [ts], as in *jam2-caa4*. There are more radical changes between borrowings and the Cantonese sources in terms of intonation, as Cantonese tones are not preserved. Instead, all syllables receive stress and they are uttered at a high-level pitch. This process of borrowing in Hong Kong English is therefore different from code-switching, in which speakers do not modify the pronunciation of the item from the original Cantonese. Code-switching is the subject of Chapter 5.

A loanword from Chinese or Cantonese may be combined with another English word, resulting in a loan-blend; for example, *Ching Ming Festival* (a Chinese festival in mid-spring, when people pay tribute to deceased ancestors), in which *Ching Ming* is borrowed from Cantonese and *Festival* is an English word or morpheme.

Loan translations, or calques, are a special type of borrowing. In our context, they refer to expressions borrowed from Cantonese or Chinese where the Cantonese morphemes are translated into English without traits of Cantonese pronunciation. In a way, these loan translations are more integrated into English and their Cantonese origin is more opaque compared with the non-translated borrowings. For instance, the area north of the Kowloon Peninsula and the outlying islands in Hong Kong is called 'the New Territories' (san1 gaai3). The two Chinese characters新界 (san1 gaai3) literally mean 'new' and 'territories' respectively. On the other hand, the name *Hong Kong* is not a loan translation but simply a phonetic transliteration of the two Chinese characters 香港 (hoeng1 gong2), which is the Chinese name of Hong Kong. These two syllables, after being transliterated into English, cannot be decomposed into any meaningful morphemes in English. Taking the example further, a possible loan translation of *Hong Kong* is 'Fragrance Harbour', and indeed the meaning of *Hong Kong* is usually translated as 'Fragrant Harbour'.

In the following examples, we classify some of the commonly used Chinese loanwords in Hong Kong English into the following categories: (a) cultural practices; (b) food and beverage items; (c) leisure activities; (d) community activities; and (e) others.

(a) Cultural practices

Ching Ming (Festival)	a spring festival to sweep the graves
Chung Yeung (Festival)	an autumn festival to commemorate ancestors
Mid-Autumn Festival	a festival in the middle of autumn to worship the moon
Tin Hau Festival	a festival honouring Tin Hau, the goddess of the sea
dragon boat	a narrow boat with a dragon head, used in racing during the Tuen Ng Festival
fung shui	literally 'wind and water'; it refers to the environment of a place, which affects people living or working there
kung hei fat choy	a common congratulatory saying exchanged during the Chinese New Year
laisee	red packet money (see *red packet* below)
lion dance	a performance staged by martial art practitioners dressed up as a lion
red packet	same as *laisee*, that is, a small red paper packet used to carry a money gift. *Red packet* is a loan translation from an expression for his object, namely, *hung4-fung1-baau1* (紅封包), literally 'red packet'.

(b) Food and beverage items

baak choy	Chinese cabbage (also *bak choy*)
beggar's chicken	chicken baked in lotus leaves and clay
bird's nest	swallow's nests
cha/chaa	Chinese tea
char-siu	roasted pork
dim-sum	snacks served at Chinese restaurants during the day time
egg tart	a local Hong Kong snack which Chris Patten, the ex-governor, was reportedly very fond of

faat choy	black hair-like seaweed (*faat* literally means 'hair')
fishball	a popular local snack made of fish meat
lychee	a kind of fruit
wonton	a kind of Chinese dumpling stuffed with minced pork
mooncake	a Chinese cake made of ground lotus seed and egg yolk which is eaten to celebrate the Mid-Autumn Festival

(c) Leisure activities

kung fu	Chinese martial arts
mahjong	a Chinese game with four people using small tiles imprinted with symbols, usually involving gambling
tai chi	a kind of kung fu, but slower in motion
yum cha	literally *drink tea*, this always refers to lunch with dim-sum and rice or noodle dishes in Chinese restaurants

(d) Community activities

black society	triad society
boat people	boat dwellers or Vietnamese refugees
coolie	an unskilled labourer
fishball girls	a type of sex worker
kaifong	literally a 'street square', used to refer to a neighbourhood
lap sap	rubbish or refuse; the name *Lap Sap Chung* was created to mean 'Litter Bug'
snakehead	the leader of a human smuggling ring
taipan	the head of a business company

(e) Others

Canto-	abbreviation for *Cantonese* (e.g. Canto-pop)
gweilo	literally *ghost people*, this refers to non-Chinese 'westerners', and is derogatory if not discriminatory. The non-Chinese westerners in Hong Kong have adopted it as a term to describe themselves.

Many place names in Hong Kong English are borrowed from Cantonese. Some examples follow, many of which are also names for stations along the Mass Transit Railway (MTR) line as announced in English.[3] These names are familiar to both Chinese and expatriates in Hong Kong, and they are also widely used with standardised English spellings in printed texts[4] such as the *South China Morning Post*, and internet communication among Hong Kong people.

> *Hong Kong, Kowloon, Lantau, Pokfulam, Wanchai, Cheung Chau, Tsim Sha Tsui, Hunghom, Kowloon Tong, Shatin, Taipo, Homantin, Mongkok, Wanchai, Sheung Wan, Cheung Sha Wan, Lan Kwai Fong, Shamshuipo, Ma On Shan, Chap Lap Kok (Chep Lap Kok or Chek Lap Kok), Sai Kung, North Point, Clear Water Bay.*

A number of these names are phonetically transliterated from Chinese, such as *Pokfulam, Hunghom, Shatin, Mongkok* and so on. These place names do not have any meaningful reference to speakers of other varieties of English. Some place names, on the other hand, are loan translation, such as *North Point* and *Clear Water Bay*. These names mean exactly the same in both Chinese and English, and the meaning is accessible to other speakers of English.

4.10 Coinage, abbreviations and acronyms

Coinage refers to the creation of a new word or expression for a new concept or entity. One example in Hong Kong English is *benchmark examination*, which refers to an English test the government set up for practising English teachers in primary and secondary schools. Bolton (2003: 212) gives the examples of *mini-halls*, which refers to private apartments rented by university students, and *hallmates*, which refers to fellow classmates living in the same hall of residence.

Many proper names referring to institutions, occupations and buildings can be considered examples of coinage. An example of coinage in the name of an institution is the English newspaper in Hong Kong, the *South China Morning Post*. These names may undergo a further process by being reduced to abbreviations; for example, the *South China Morning Post* is commonly referred to as the *SCMP*. However, although abbreviations are productive in Hong Kong English, they seem to be specific to certain names. For instance, the other English newspaper in Hong Kong, the *Hong Kong Standard*, no longer available in print format, was never known as the *HKS*, and whereas *Radio Television of Hong Kong*, the government-run radio station, is known as *RTHK*, *Metro Radio* is never referred to as *MR*.

Where occupations in the Hong Kong government are concerned, the abbreviations *AO* (administrative officer) and *EO* (executive officer) are well known. However, the chief executive is seldom called the *CE*, and the financial secretary is not alternatively known as the *FS*. In the private sector, *OL* ('office lady') is a popular abbreviation, but neither *OB* ('office boy') nor *OM* ('office man') seems to exist. The International Financial Centre in Central, now the highest building in Hong Kong, is abbreviated to the *IFC*. However, Pacific Place, an office-mall complex nearby in Admiralty similar to IFC, is never referred to as *PP*.

The following list contains some of the more popular abbreviations in Hong Kong English, most of which are related to public institutions such as transport, public utilities, university and colleges. Again, some degree of specificity applies in all these domains; that is, not every bank or school with an English name has an abbreviation in current use. There are also some abbreviations which do not refer to public institutions (that is, *Others* in the list below).

(a) Banks
   BOC   Bank of China
   HSBC   Hong Kong Shanghai Banking Corporation

(b) Transport
   KCR   Kowloon–Canton Railway (now part of the MTR)
   KMB   Kowloon Motor Bus
   MTR   Mass Transit Railway (corresponds to the London Underground or New York Subway)

(c) Government or public utilities
   EMB   Education and Manpower Bureau
   HA   Hospital Authority
   ICAC   Independent Commission Against Corruption
   SAR   Special Administrative Region

(d) Public utilities
   CLP   China Light and Power
   PCCW   Pacific Century Cable and Wireless

(e) Education
   HKCEE   Hong Kong Certificate of Education Examination
   HKUE   Hong Kong Use of English

(f) Universities and colleges
   APA   Academy of Performing Arts
   CUHK   Chinese University of Hong Kong

DBS Diocesan Boys' College
DGS Diocesan Girls' College
HKU Hong Kong University (used mostly in print)
IVE Institute of Vocational Education
QC Queen's College
SPACE School of Professional and Continuing Education
UST University of Science and Technology

(g) Others
 ABC American-born Chinese
 BBC British-born Chinese

Bauer (1983) distinguishes between abbreviations and acronyms. Whereas both are formed by taking the initial letters of words in a phrase, abbreviations are pronounced by spelling out a series of English letters, whereas acronyms are pronounced as one English word. Examples of acronyms in Hong Kong English include *NET* (Native English teachers), *SPACE* (School of Professional and Continuing Education) and *IVE* (Institution of Vocational Education).

In some instances, names do not have abbreviations or acronyms in current use, but they may be somewhat reduced or shortened. Taking names for universities as an illustration, *City University of Hong Kong* is not called *CUHK*, because that abbreviation is used to stand for the *Chinese University of Hong Kong*. Consequently, the former university is referred to as *CityU*. What is interesting is that the Chinese University of Hong Kong may be called *Chinese U* too. When both an abbreviation and a shortened form are available, the mode of discourse (that is, spoken or written communication) seems to play a role as to which one is to be used. For example, the abbreviation *HKU* (Hong Kong University) is used in print, but the shortened form *Hong Kong U* is used in spoken conversation.

4.11 Blending and compounding

New words can also be formed by combining two existing words through blending and compounding. These two processes are found to be productive in Hong Kong English, too.

In blending, a new word is formed by reducing two words and combining the two parts (Bauer 1983). Examples in Hong Kong English include *Legco* (Legislative Council), *Exco* (Executive Council), *Cantopop* (Cantonese popular songs) and *Chinglish* (Chinese-English, which may refer to code-switching or English with Chinese characteristics; a derogatory term).

In compounding, new words or expressions are formed by combining two or more existing words without reduction. Some examples in Hong Kong English are listed as follows:

> *lemon tea* Tea which may be hot or iced, to which slices of lemon are added instead of milk. (Tea served this way was once popular in the UK, but it is much less common now.)
>
> *tea buffet* This is not a buffet of various kinds of tea, but a buffet of snacks, desserts and drinks for afternoon tea.
>
> *tea set* This does not refer to a set of cups or tableware, but afternoon tea with specific snacks such as French toast, chicken wings, noodles and so on.

It is possible that *lemon tea* and *tea set* are loan translations from the Cantonese expressions *ling4-mung1 caa4* (literally 'lemon tea') and *caa4 caan1* (literally 'tea meal' or 'tea set') respectively.

4.12 Affixation

Both derivational and inflectional suffixes are commonly found in Hong Kong English. In derivation, new words are formed by adding affixes (such as *-er*) to existing words. Some derived words appear to be specific to Hong Kong English; for example, *Hongkonger* (a Hong Kong person) and *mainlander* (a person from mainland China). Although the *-er* is a common derivational suffix in English, the resulting lexical items are unique to Hong Kong English because the stems are typically Hong Kong English.

Similarly, English inflectional suffixation, which involves the addition of suffixes such as the plural suffix *-s* or the past tense suffix *-ed*, are very productive in Hong Kong English, too. For example, the plural form of the loanword *gweilo* is *gweilos*. However, some uncountable or collective nouns in British English tend to be treated as countable nouns to which may be added the plural suffix in Hong Kong English; for instance, *equipments* and *staffs* (Bolton 2003: 213). In section 3.6, this is attributed to the influence of Cantonese, in which there is no grammatical distinction between mass nouns and count nouns; accordingly, speakers mark an English mass or collective noun with a plural marker when they construe it as countable (that is, *equipment* is understood as one piece of equipment; *staff* is understood as one staff member).

4.13 Lexical choice

Some Hong Kong English expressions are also found in British English or other Englishes, but they tend to be used in specific contexts in Hong Kong English where other expressions would be used in these varieties. For instance, in Hong Kong universities, restaurants are usually known as *canteens, student canteens, staff canteens* or *staff restaurant*, whereas in British universities, although the word *canteen* may be used, food outlets appear to be more commonly referred to by a wider set of words, such as *café, cafeteria, bar, lounge, snack bar, food court* or *refectory*, and the term *restaurant* tends to be used for outside establishments.

4.14 Semantic change

Some expressions in Hong Kong English have developed meanings or connotations which are absent in other varieties of English. For instance, *shopping* carries the connotation of women buying fashion products, and it may involve real transactions or just window shopping. The term is seldom used in Hong Kong English to refer to housewives buying food or other household goods in supermarkets. In British English, a *podium* usually refers to a platform for conductors or public speakers, but in Hong Kong a *podium* means a large area in many universities which is mid-level between the car park and the classrooms and where most facilities such as banks, cafés, bookshops and library entrances are located. Accordingly, the lifts in academic buildings have a button for the *P (podium)* floor. Another example is the use of *shroff* to refer to the kiosk where payment for parking is made in car parks in Hong Kong. The word originally means, according to the *OED*, 'a banker or money-changer in the East; in the Far East, a native expert employed to detect bad coin'.

Bolton (2003: 288–97) lists a number of further examples which fall into this category. For example, *uncle* and *auntie* refer to friends of parents instead of their siblings; *harsh* comes to be used to describe people who are demanding on others; *Christians* refers to Protestants exclusively in opposition to *Catholics*.

4.15 Hong Kong English vocabulary in computer-mediated communication

The examples of Hong Kong English vocabulary in the sections above are likely to be more well-known ones which are found in all-English texts such as newspapers (for example, the *South China Morning Post* – see

Taylor 1989; Carless 1995; Chow 2001) or other genres such as novels and weblogs (see examples in Cummings 2007). These texts may be authored by Hong Kong Chinese, or by native speakers of English who have acquired a fair knowledge of Hong Kong. Many recent works on computer-mediated communication involving Hong Kong Chinese speakers have documented a lot more English expressions either borrowed or translated from Cantonese (Chan 1999; Fung and Carter 2007a; Ho 2006; Lee 2007), but there is some reservation as to whether they should be properly treated as Hong Kong English. That is, the participants in these internet exchanges are Cantonese–English bilinguals, and many of these borrowed items or translations seem to be highly contextualised and ad hoc, with their meaning sometimes opaque to outsiders or even the addressees (Fung and Carter 2007a). Accordingly, one may wonder whether these expressions are better described as some kind of code-mixing or code-switching (see Chapter 5 for code-mixing with English in Hong Kong). In any event, some of the more common expressions in these data may eventually become core vocabulary in Hong Kong English. The following are some candidates attested in various datasets (Chan 1999; Fung and Carter 2007a; Ho 2006; Lee 2007).

add oil	an expression of encouragement, translated from *gaa1-jau2*（加油）
blow water	to speak without substance, translated from *ceoi1-seoi2*（吹水）
sky and earth lesson	classes scheduled far apart in early morning and late afternoon, leaving a long break between the classes, translated from *tin1-dei6-tong4*（天地堂）
ma fan	troublesome, borrowed from *maa4-faan4*（麻煩）
mo liu	describes somebody who feels bored or does silly things, translated from *mou4-liu4*（無聊）

4.16 Examples of Hong Kong English vocabulary in our data

Our data do not contain many examples of Hong Kong English vocabulary, but the following are some expressions attested when the speakers are describing their happy events.

(32) erm my parents used to take me to the <u>Lantau</u> Island

{05-HE:00:18}

(33) and that amusement park was called . . . <u>Lee Yuen</u>

{10-HE:00:21}

(34) yes er and ... after the night time on the other day we have some <u>mass game</u>

{09-HE:01:52}

(35) so er there are some like er ... <u>pirate ship</u> er <u>pirate</u> ... <u>boat</u>

{10-HE:01:26}

(36) there's another big one that's called <u>Ocean Park</u>

{10-HE:02:32}

(37) er especially ... the weather in Hong Kong is quite hot so we always kept in a <u>air con</u> room

{09-HE:08:38}

(38) and it was so nice 'cause you would pass through er like <u>country houses</u>

{05-HE:01:06}

(39) it's like we've got a <u>cottage</u> or something like that there

{05-HE:03:23}

In extracts (32) and (33), we have examples of borrowing from Cantonese, in which the pronunciation is similar to the original. *Lantau* (32) refers to an outlying island south-west of Hong Kong Island. It was previously a rural area, but recent developments have made it the location of the Hong Kong international airport and Hong Kong Disneyland. *Lantau* was in fact borrowed from an older name in Cantonese, that is, *laan6-tau4* (爛頭), as the island is more popularly known as *daai6-jyu4-saan1* (大嶼山) in Cantonese. The word *Lantau* is pronounced in such a way that both of the syllables are stressed with a high-level pitch.[5] *Lee Yuen* in example (33) is borrowed from Cantonese *lai6-jyun2* (荔園), and refers to a theme park closed in 1997. As for *Lantau*, the two syllables of *Lee Yuen* are both stressed. What is more, there are changes in the vowels; [laɪjyn] in the Cantonese source expression was pronounced as [lijɛn]. A further point of interest is that *Lee Yuen* is not an established loanword like *Hong Kong* or *Lantau*, and Speaker 10 appears to produce [lʊɪ] before she corrects it to [li], presumably reckoning that [lʊɪ] will not be understood by the interviewer.

Mass game in extract (34) is an example of a borrowing that translates the Cantonese words rather than using the original pronunciation. It does not refer to any particular sport, but to a group game or activity which people play for fun or entertainment in camps or gatherings. This expression is supposedly taken from the Chinese phrase *zaap6-tai2 jau4-hei3* (集體遊戲), literally, *collective game*. In example (35), *pirate ship* (or *pirate boat*) refers to a large swinging boat for rides in amusement parks, presumably translated from the Cantonese expression *hoi2-dou6 syun4* (海盜船), which literally means *pirate ship*, and which is itself an instance of semantic extension, although this expression is known in other varieties of English as well (for example, there are swinging pirate ships in many UK amusement parks).

There are also examples in which the names for places in Hong Kong are not necessarily borrowings from Cantonese, but could be examples of coinage. For instance, *Ocean Park* in extract (36) is the English name for a theme park in Aberdeen, Hong Kong Island, a popular tourist spot and a competitor to Disneyland. This name is closely matched by the Cantonese name, *hoi2-joeng4 gung1-jyun2* (海洋公園), literally *Ocean Park*, and could therefore be a loan translation, if it was indeed translated from the Chinese name. However, it is likely that the Chinese name and the English name were coined at the same time that the Ocean Park Corporation was set up.

An example of a blend can be seen in *air con* in extract (37), which is a shortened form of 'air conditioned', also observed by Bolton (2003: 288).

We also have instances of semantic change in our data. In example (38), *country house* does not refer to a big house belonging to rich people or aristocrats, as the term is normally conceived in Britain. Instead, it refers to a much smaller house which is found in the countryside areas of Hong Kong, usually three storeys high and occupied by several families or units; in Cantonese this kind of dwelling is called *cyun1-uk1* (村屋), literally *village house*. It is most probable that Speaker 5 was referring to the same kind of house when she used the word *cottage* later on in the conversation in extract (39). Again, a *cottage* in Hong Kong is not identical to a cottage in Britain (which is normally a small dwelling occupied by one unit or family), but is a building divided into several apartments and rented to different families or units. In sum, the meaning of *country house* and *cottage* has changed, and both expressions converge to refer to the same kind of house.

4.17 Summary

In this chapter, we have shown that DMs such as *actually* and *because–so* have distinctive patterns of use in the spoken variety, and that there are some similarities between Hong Kong English and varieties such as Singapore English in features like utterance-final particles and topic–comment sentences. We have indicated that more work needs to be done to ascertain whether similar patterns can be found in written Hong Kong English.

Concerning vocabulary, we have demonstrated how new lexical items have come into use in Hong Kong English through processes such as coinage, affixation and borrowing, with Cantonese acting as a rich source of lexis.

In the next chapter, we look at an area related to that of lexical borrowing: code-switching in Hong Kong English.

Notes

1. Literally, 'I seek you'.

2. See section 1.2, Chapter 1, for information on the romanisation system used here.

3. Public announcements in MTR trains are usually trilingual: in Cantonese, English and Putonghua.

4. In the list, *Chap Lap Kok (Chep Lap Kok* or *Chek Lap Kok)* shows alternative spellings, probably because the place has become famous only in relatively recent times.

5. Interestingly, the interviewer, who supposedly had not come across the word before, repeated it in a follow-up question, but only stressed the first syllable.

5 Code-switching

The previous chapter discusses borrowing from Cantonese to Hong Kong English, noting that loanwords may undergo phonological adaptation to English. In this connection, it is interesting to find the following excerpt in the data of Speaker 5.

(1) *Context:* Speaker 5 was recalling her classmate who came from a wealthy family. The family was so rich that there was a cook in the house and family members took turns to order food for dinner.

1	05:	and then I think erm he said yesterday I order erm
2	Int:	((laughs))
3	05:	barbecue er . . . um pork something like that
4	Int:	uhuh uhuh
5	05:	roast pork
6	Int:	uhuh
7	05:	and then er but then in Chinese in Cantonese he em he used the
8		term *mat6 zap1 caa1 siu1* [honey-sauce barbecued pork] but in my
9		family we only say *caa1 siu1* [barbecued pork] every time
10	Int:	mhm
11	05:	every time we we won't describe the first part the first part
12	Int:	uhuh
13	05:	is about a barbecue sauce
14	Int:	uhuh uhuh
15	05:	the roasted one but my parents never said something like that
16	Int:	uhuh
17	05:	they they only say the pork
18	Int:	yeah yeah
19	05:	((unintelligible)) these two words so um in my mind I still
20		remember that clearly cause in Cantonese we've got a lots of
21		words with erm exactly the same sound same sounds but different
22		meanings
23	Int:	yeah

24 05:   so that the first word *mat6* [honey or melon] is similar er is
25   actually the same sound as um the melon
26   Int: mhm . . . melon

{05-HE:08:05–09:09}

The three expressions *mat6 zap1 caa1 siu1* (honey-sauce barbecued pork; line 8), *caa1 siu1* (barbecued pork; line 9) and *mat6* (honey, also melon; see lines 24 and 25) were pronounced with clear Cantonese tones. In addition, Speaker 5 made it clear that she was speaking Cantonese for these expressions (line 7 and 20), which implies her awareness that English was and should be the language of the ongoing interaction, and she was departing from it only temporarily. Accordingly, example (1) seems a better illustration not so much of borrowing as of code-switching, the use of two (or more) languages in the same communicative situation (Gumperz 1982; Heller 1988; Milroy and Muysken 1995; Romaine 1995).

In this chapter, we look at some of the issues in code-switching in Hong Kong.

5.1 Borrowing, code-mixing and code-switching

It has to be noted that the terms 'borrowing', 'code-switching' and 'code-mixing' are used in a notoriously confusing way in the bilingualism literature, with different definitions given by different researchers (Gardner-Chloros 2009). As mentioned above and in Chapter 4, borrowing refers to words taken from another language which undergo phonological assimilation and perhaps morphological assimilation (for example, *mooncake* undergoes English plural marking and becomes *mooncakes*) to the borrowing language. Code-mixing or code-switching undergoes less integration into the base language and involves various units, from single words to longer elements such as phrases or even clauses (Grosjean 1982; Romaine 1995). Integration into the base language or the borrowing language, however, is relative, and therefore code-switching and borrowing are better conceived as two ends of a continuum rather than two discrete categories (Myers-Scotton 1993b).

There is another criterion for distinguishing borrowing from code-switching or code-mixing. Borrowed items are supposed to be so deeply entrenched into the base language that speakers are not always conscious of their foreign origin (Grosjean 1982). In code-switching or code-mixing, participants are aware that two different languages are being used (as in example (1) above) for various communicative functions. In example (1), the Cantonese expressions *mat6 zap1 caa1 siu1* (honey-sauce barbecued pork; line 8) and *caal siul* (barbecued pork; line 9) were used by the classmate's family and the speaker's family respectively, and therefore in both cases code-switching marks quotations, which is quite common in different bilingual communities (B. Chan 2004; Gumperz 1982). The pragmatic function of code-switching here may well be *contextualization* (Gumperz 1982), that is, highlighting the fact that these Cantonese expressions had actually been uttered in another context by herself and other speakers, and Speaker 5 was only quoting them in the ongoing interaction. In lines 19–25, Speaker 5 was explaining why she could not understand the Cantonese expression *mat6 zapl caal siul* (honey-sauce barbecued pork; line 8); that is, she could not grasp the meaning of *mat6* (honey or melon), which was ambiguous in Cantonese. Here, code-switching points to a Cantonese expression which the speaker had used in preceding text.

Earlier works use the term 'code-mixing' to refer to *intra*-sentential alternation of Cantonese and English in Hong Kong (Gibbons 1979, 1987; Chan 1992). However, the term has somehow been stigmatised, taken to imply that the bilingual speakers are 'semilinguals' of some kind, who are incompetent in either or both of the languages. Luke and Richards (1982), for example, suggested that 'code-mixing' indicates the 'middle-level proficiency' of English of Hong Kong Chinese speakers. This kind of perception is biased because intra-sentential alternation of languages is a common feature in the speech of bilinguals around the world, irrespective of their second language proficiency (Romaine 1995). On the other hand, 'code-switching' was used to refer to *inter*-sentential alternations of languages, which is apparently not so common among Hong Kong speakers (Chen 2008; Luke 1998). Looking at the sociolinguistics literature outside Hong Kong, however, one finds that 'code-switching' has been more commonly used as a general term which covers both intra-sentential and inter-sentential alternation of languages, and it has been so used especially in influential monographs or anthologies (see Auer 1998; Grosjean 1982; Gumperz 1982; Heller 1988; Milroy and Muysken 1995; Myers-Scotton 1993a, 1993b, 2002; Romaine 1995 and so on). Some Hong Kong researchers have seemingly followed the trend and used 'code-switching' instead of 'code-mixing' to refer to intra-sentential alternation of Cantonese and English (for example, Chan 1998b, 2003; Li 1999, 2000, 2001). For the sake of simplicity, we use 'code-switching' below essentially to refer to both inter-sentential and intra-sentential alternation of Cantonese and English, while noting that many works, earlier ones in particular, actually use the term 'code-mixing' for intra-sentential alternation of the two languages.

5.2 Code-switching in Hong Kong

The vitality of code-switching in Hong Kong is most wittily illustrated in Li and Tse (2002). In their experiment, a dozen university students deliberately refrained from speaking any English for one day, and then they shared their experiences in a follow-up group interview. All of those students who attended the interview reported that they were embarrassed by communication breakdown and they found it virtually impossible to interact in pure Cantonese. One of them remarked somewhat jokingly, 'I felt that if someone were to kill most of the Hongkongers, specifying that no English was allowed, then many people would have been killed'; another student concurred immediately, 'I'd be the first one to die' (Li and Tse 2002: 181).

In fact, it is not only students or adolescents who engage in extensive code-switching with Cantonese and English. It is true that most studies draw data from university students, who are probably most accessible to researchers who work in universities (Fung and Carter 2007a, 2007b; Gibbons 1987; Li and Tse 2002; Leung 2001), but data have also been gathered from both adults and children, including working professionals (Leung 1987; Reynolds 1985), bilingual children (Lai 2006; Yip and Matthews 2007; Yiu 2005) and secondary school teachers (Johnson 1983; Lin 1996). Chen (2008) examines code-switching in adolescents of approximately the same age as university students, but her informants are 'returnees' who emigrated to English-speaking countries and whose 'code-mixing style' is distinguishable from that of local Hong Kong Chinese. In brief, in the English of returnees, there is more intersentential alternation, which involves longer elements such as English phrases and sentences.

Code-switching is attested not only in everyday communication but also in all kinds of discourse in Hong Kong, including written texts and the print media (Yau 1993). While the majority of works are indeed based on spoken data in spontaneous conversation (for example, Chan 1998a; Gibbons 1979, 1987; Luke 1998), others have explored code-switching in different registers or genres such as classroom discourse (Lin 1996), stand-up comedy (Tsang and Wong 2004), newspapers (Li 1996, 1998, 2001), fashion magazines (Lee 2000), poster advertisements (Lock 2003) and pop songs (Chan 2009). More recently, there has been a lot of interest in electronic communication, where code-switching is prevalent (Chan 1999; Fung and Carter 2007a; Ho 2006; Lee 2007). None the less, these studies (except Chan 1999) have little discussion of Hong Kong English.

There has been a keen interest in code-switching in Hong Kong. The literature consists of not only research monographs and journal articles by professional linguists but also numerous theses or dissertations, which indicates how popular the topic has been among graduate students. A brief survey from early studies, such as Gibbons (1979), to very recent ones, such as Chen (2008), reveals a variety of concerns and approaches to the topic. Whereas most studies focus on why bilingual speakers code-switch at all – in other words, the motivations for code-switching (for example, Li 1996, 1998, 2000, 2001; Li and Tse 2002; Luke 1998) – there have been some attempts to analyse the grammatical patterns of code-switching in a more formal perspective (see Chan 1998a, 1998b, 2003; Leung 2001).

Despite the pervasiveness of code-switching, particularly intra-sentential code-switching, in Hong Kong and a great deal of scholarship devoted to the topic, the overwhelming majority of works focus on communication among Hong Kong Chinese who interact in Cantonese (Chan 1998a; Gibbons 1987; Li and Tse 2002). In contrast, few studies have investigated code-switching where the base language is English in the ongoing exchange. This may well be due to the fact that code-switching is seldom used in such encounters, as English is still used very much in out-group communication in Hong Kong where non-Cantonese-speaking expatriates generally know little Cantonese (such as example (1) above). In addition, English is used in more formal situations (such as public speech or meetings) where code-switching is less appropriate, considering the fact that code-switching tends to be common in informal communication within peers (Gumperz 1982; Myers-Scotton 1993a).

5.3 The morphosyntax of code-switching and Hong Kong English

Code-switching in Hong Kong is usually intra-sentential among Chinese who speak Cantonese with their families, peers and in everyday communication, with English words and phrases embedded into an essentially Cantonese sentence structure. Where code-switching involves single English words, they are predominantly lexical, that is, nouns, verbs, adjectives and adverbs (Chan 1998a, 1998b, 2003; Leung 2001). Conversely, Cantonese contributes both content and function words, as well as bound morphemes, to the code-switched sentence. In terms of the Matrix Language Frame Model (Myers-Scotton 1993b, 2002), Cantonese acts as the 'matrix language' whereas English acts as the 'embedded language'. Some examples follow.[1]

> (2) keoi5 zeoi3-hau6 dou1 *keep* dou2 go2   go3   *promise* (verb, noun)
>   he/she finally   also keep   able DEM   CL   promise
>   'At last, he was able to keep that promise.'
> (*The New Generation on Fire* (Fo2-Jit6-San1-Sai3-Doi6/火熱新世代), Metro
> Radio, Info Channel)

(3) jyu4-gwo2 zing3-fu2   jau5   mat1   *counter-proposal* ... (noun)
    If   government   has   what   counter-proposal ...
    'If the government has any counter-proposal ...'
        (News report, Television Broadcasting Company, Jade Channel)

(4) go2   go3 zyu2 je5   ge3   fong1-faat3 hai6 hou2 *effective* (adjective)
    DEM CL   cook thing LNK method   COP EMP effective
    'That method of cooking is very effective.'
(*So Far So Good* (So-Far-蘇-Good), Television Broadcasting Company, Jade
                                                              Channel)

(5) ji5-cin4 di1 jan4 hai6 *exactly* gam2 joeng2   heoi3 hang6-saan1 (adverb)
    Past   CL man COP exactly this   appearance go   hiking
    'People in the past were exactly like this when they went hiking.'
(*Playing around Kansai* (Waan4-Jau4-Gwan1-Sai1/頑遊關西), Television
                                    Broadcasting Company, Jade Channel)

Longer elements of English in code-switching involve various phrases
or compound words, as extract (6) below. Sometimes, a whole phrase
(for example, extract (7) or (8)) or even a clause in English may be code-
switched (for example, extract (9)).

(6) keoi5 hai6 jat1 go3 *internet culture* ge3   zit3-muk6 (compound noun)
    It   COP one CL internet culture LNK programme
    'It is a programme about internet culture.'
(*Forests and Blogs* (Jyun4-Lam4-Bou6-Lok6/原林部落), Radio Television
                                            Hong Kong, Channel 2)

(7) wui5   jau5 jat1 di1 san1 go1   *for worship* (prepositional phrase)
     Will   have one CL   new song   for   worship
     '(In the gathering, there) will be some new songs for worship.'
                                                    (B. Chan 2004)

(8) nei5 jiu3   *passionate about your job* (adjective phrase)
     You   have-to   passionate about your job
     'You have to be passionate about your job.'
                        (Advertisement, Commercial Radio, Channel 881)

(9) keoi5   seng4-jat6   dou1   waa6   *keep searching for a girl* (clause)
     he/she   always   also   say   keep searching for a girl
     'He always says (he) keeps searching for a girl (that is, a girlfriend).'
                                                        (Chan 1998a)

These data are vastly different from example (1), in which English is the matrix language according to the Matrix Language Frame Model (Myers-Scotton 1993b), with Cantonese words or phrases inserted into an English-framed sentence. Extracted below are the code-switched sentences from our data, in which Cantonese nouns or noun phrases are embedded into an English sentence.

(10) but then in Chinese in Cantonese he em he used the term *mat6 zap1 caa1 siu1* [honey-sauce barbecued pork] but in my family we only say *caa1 siu1* [barbecued pork] every time

                                                        {05-HE:08:28}

(11) so that the first word *mat6* [honey or melon] is similar er is actually the same sound as um the melon

                                                        {05-HE:09:00}

Data in which English is the matrix language are sometimes found among speakers whose English is more dominant in terms of higher proficiency or higher frequency of use, such as Chen's 'returnees' (2008) and some bilingual children (Yiu 2005). The following example was produced by a 'returnee' who was raised in an English-speaking country.

(12) I live with *gau2- zai2 bi4-bi1* [baby dog, or puppy] and my *tung4-uk1* [housemate]

                                                        (Chan 1998a)

The returnees are none the less able to adjust to different code-mixing styles, producing more Cantonese-framed sentences with local Hong Kong people but more English-framed sentences with other returnees (Chen 2008).

Although most code-switching data in Hong Kong are attested where Cantonese is the base language of the ongoing interaction and often the matrix language of code-switching (such as examples (2) to (9); Chan 1998a, 1998b; Leung 2001), and thus are not to be equated with Hong Kong English, where English is the matrix language in code-switching (such as examples (10), (11); and (12)), there are common morphosyntactic properties in both varieties. This is hardly surprising, since

Cantonese–English code-switching and Hong Kong English are both under the influence of Cantonese and English.

For instance, in Hong Kong English, speakers may omit the plural marker -*s* of English nouns in contexts which impose a plural reading (see section 3.1). The omission of the English plural marker is also attested in code-switching, as shown in the following example.

(13) nei5 zou6 saai3 di1 *assignment* mei6
    you do ASP CL assignment SFP
    'Have you finished those assignments?'

(Chan 1998a)

In addition to the plural marker, speakers may skip agreement markers where they would have been required in British English. This is attested in Hong Kong English (see section 3.4) and in code-switching (Chan 1998a, 1998b), such as example (14) below.

(14) go3 *goal* *guide* ngo5 dei6 di1 *nurse* heoi3 zou6 je5
    CL goal guide I PL CL nurse go do things
    'The goal guides us nurses on how to do our job.'

(Chan 1998b)

In Hong Kong English, some words may have undergone category conversion (see section 3.9), and this phenomenon is again observed in code-switching. For instance, in extract (15) below, the word *even* is not used as a pre-determiner in a noun phrase (for example, '[*Even a child*] noun phrase *can do that*') according to English grammar; rather, it is used as a subordinator with the meaning of *although* or *even though*.

(15) *Even* nei5 mou5 je5 zou6, zing3-fu2 dou1 wui5 bei2 di1 cin2 nei5
    even you NEG thing do government also will give some money you
    'Even though you don't have a job, the government will give you some money.'

(Chan 1992)

In example (16) below, the word *even* is similarly used as a subordinator in Hong Kong English.

(16) so even you go very away from the cities you still find a lot of people
    {09-HE:08:08}

In example (17) below, the English preposition *through* behaves as a verb which is suffixed with an aspect marker in Cantonese (that is, *zo2*). A similar change from preposition to verb is attested in Hong Kong English, as noted in section 3.9. Example (18) repeats example (106) in section 3.9.

(17) ngo5 hai6 *through* zo2 XXXX   sik1   dak1 YYY
     I   COP through ASP [name of an organisation] know PRT [name]
     'I got to know YYY through XXXX.'
               (*Power of Beauty* (Mei2-Lai6-Lik6-Loeng6/美麗力量), Television
                                          Broadcasting Company, Jade Channel)

(18) just alonged it
                                          {05-MT: 06:21}

5.4 Code-switching as an agent of nativisation in Hong Kong English

Notwithstanding similarities and differences in form, Cantonese–English code-switching does have a significant contribution to make in the development of Hong Kong English. More specifically, code-switching has provided a pathway along which English comes to be used among Hong Kong Chinese speakers in more informal or intimate domains, such as with peers and in everyday communication. Whereas English is still considered to be a foreign language, inappropriate for intra-ethnic communication (Li 1999), code-switching seems to have neutralised the 'alien-ness' or 'other-ness' of English. This process of indigenisation or nativisation of English has recently speeded up with electronic communication, where Hong Kong Chinese speakers use much more English among themselves with extensive code-switching (Chan 1999; Fung and Carter 2007a; Ho 2006; Lee 2007); Pang (2003) sees it as a cradle fostering local norms of English, leading to the emergence of Hong Kong English (see section 6.4).

In Schneider's (2003, 2007) typology, nativisation of the English language is seen as crucial for the emergence of New Englishes. A survey of the status and development of Hong Kong English is given in the next chapter.

Note

1. Abbreviations for the grammatical categories in the literal translations given in the examples are as follows: ASP = aspect marker, CL = classifier, COP = copular verb, DEM = demonstrative, EMP = emphatic marker, LNK= linker or linking particle, NEG = negation marker, PL = plural marker, PRT = particle, SFP = sentence-final particle.

6 Hong Kong English: a sociolinguistic history

The interest in Hong Kong English as a variety is a relatively recent phenomenon, and its status is very much under dispute (see section 6.4 below). Because of this, there has been little, if any, documentation of historical language change. Empirically, there have been few studies which describe the formal linguistic properties of Hong Kong English in great detail (in comparison with, say, Singapore English); this, coupled with the emergent status of the variety, means it is virtually impossible to compare two datasets collected at different times for varietal differences. In addition, work on Hong Kong English, other than that which looks at it as a learner language, did not really start in earnest until Luke and Richards' groundbreaking research in 1982. Change, as far as Hong Kong English is concerned, has almost exclusively focused on the social status of English, or the changing status of English with reference to spoken Cantonese and written Standard Chinese in the Hong Kong context.

This chapter surveys the sociolinguistic history of English in Hong Kong. The description leads on to a discussion concerning the emergence of Hong Kong English as a new variety. This is intended to contextualise the preceding chapters of the book, which primarily describe the formal linguistic aspects of Hong Kong English.

6.1 English in pre-colonial Hong Kong (pre-1842)

Probably the most comprehensive description of the early development of English in Hong Kong is to be found in Bolton (2003), specifically chapter 3, in which he surveys the situation between the mid-seventeenth and twentieth centuries. Bolton indicates that, before the Opium Wars, contact between westerners and Chinese in the coastal areas including Hong Kong was purely trade-based. The English used then was a form of pidgin English (Bolton 2003: 178–89; Bauer and Benedict 1997: 349–50), documented in such works as Peter

Mundy's *Travels* in the seventeenth century. Later, at the beginning of the nineteenth century, British and American Protestant missionaries also documented the pidgin English of the region (Bolton 2003); it is noted by one such missionary that 'English is the only medium of conversation between foreigners and Chinese' (Williams 1836: 431), with the inducement for this being trade, but that the Chinese were unable to understand 'good' English (Williams 1836: 431), meaning the English spoken by foreigners between themselves. The missionaries also note that not many westerners were learning Chinese because of the perceived difficulty of the language (Bolton 2003: 151).

Following the establishment of Hong Kong as a British colony in 1843, English became the official language, and its importance began to penetrate into the various domains in society: government, law, education and employment. That English, however, was the one spoken by foreigners between themselves, and not a development of the pidgin English documented in earlier days. This does not mean that pidgin English has died out in the region, however; see Baker (1987), Baker and Mühlhäusler (1990) and Shi (1991) for works documenting Chinese Pidgin English. (Singh (2001) and Todd (1990) provide good general introductions to pidgins and creoles.)

6.2 English as a colonial language (1842–1997)

English was the only official language of government in Hong Kong for more than a hundred years, from the establishment of Hong Kong as a colony until 1974, when the government passed an Official Languages Ordinance in which Chinese was also recognised as an official language. Nevertheless, the deep-rooted importance of English as the official language still persisted throughout the 1970s and 1980s, especially in governmental and legal settings. Proceedings in most law courts, and speeches delivered in the Legislative Council, the Executive Council, the Urban Council and other government bodies, were almost exclusively in English. Official bills were printed in English in the *Gazette*, a regular official publication, which is still in existence and now called the *HKSAR Gazette*.[1] Documents within the government administration from that time are all in English (Luke and Richards 1982: 54–5).

In education, the medium of instruction (MOI) reflected the dominance of English. In the early years of colonial administration, British and American Protestant missionary education played an important part in the movement from pidgin to 'standard' English, although there was no direct equivalent to the 1835 Macaulay Minute on Indian Education (Bolton 2003), which basically adopted an 'Anglicist' policy. Even at this time, there was disagreement about the MOI in missionary schools. Bolton (2003: 192–3) reports that, in 1878, the Presbyterian Calvin W. Mateer believed that all instruction should be in Chinese, whereas opponents suggested that some if not all of the curriculum should be taught in English, often bowing to parental demands. However, only a small minority of Hongkongers were receiving education at this time, and by 1935, it was reported that only between one third and one half of school-age children were in school (Bolton 2003: 194). This led to the maintenance of pidgin English in some sections of the population, as there was no exposure amongst the uneducated to 'standard' English, but there still remained the desire to use the language in certain domains of daily life, however small. It was not until the 1970s that compulsory education was introduced.

In the 1980s, the majority of secondary schools employed English as the MOI – those doing so were referred to as EMI (English as a medium of instruction) schools – despite the fact that most secondary school leavers actually did not use much English in their work or social life, except in the business and commercial sectors, where being proficient in English was an advantage. The high prestige of English in Hong Kong springs from a belief that 'knowledge of English means financial and occupational mobility' (Luke and Richards 1982: 53). This concept was reinforced by the competitiveness of public examinations in which English was the major language used, and the fact that English was the MOI in the University of Hong Kong, the institution with the higher prestige of the two universities in Hong Kong at the time, the other being the Chinese University of Hong Kong. However, EMI was not necessarily of benefit to students; Cheng et al. (1973), for example, showed that 71 per cent of students found that using English as the MOI put a huge strain on their learning. Morrison and Liu (2000) suggest that the English of teachers in the 1980s and 1990s could itself be poor.

While Cantonese and English served different social functions, the majority of ethnic Chinese did not, and still do not, use English in their everyday life. Luke and Richards (1982: 51) refer to this situation as 'diglossia without bilingualism', in which two languages were being used in the same domain, but by separate speaker groups. Those Chinese who managed to acquire a high level of English during the time of colonial rule became elites, or joined the rising middle class. This was especially the case before compulsory education was introduced. It was through the education system that any average Hong Kong citizen had the opportunity to become bilingual, and, as mentioned above, it was in the 1970s and 1980s that the Hong Kong education system moved from an elitist one to a mass education system, and thus 'a system of *mass* (or *folk) bilingualism'* emerged (Bolton 2003: 87). Parallel institutions (media such as separate English and Cantonese radio and TV stations and newspapers) arose, catering separately for the needs of the Cantonese-speaking and English-speaking groups. There was little need for the groups to communicate with each other and learn the language of the 'other'. Just like their seventeenth-century forebears, the vast majority of the English-speaking population rarely learnt Cantonese, interacting in English with only the few elitist bilingual Hong Kong Chinese. Luke and Richards (1982: 51) describe the sociolinguistic phenomenon as 'a case of societal bilingualism in which two largely monolingual communities co-exist, with a small group of bilingual Cantonese functioning as linguistic middle men'.

Luke and Richards (1982) saw English in Hong Kong at the time as neither a foreign language nor a second language. It had official status and important social functions, and yet not many Hongkongers could speak it, or did so in the home. The situation was unlike that of Japan or Taiwan, however, as those Chinese who could speak it had an English proficiency much higher than speakers in Japan or Taiwan, and were surrounded by English every day in a way that the Japanese and Taiwanese were not. On the other hand, English in Hong Kong had not developed its own native norms in the same way that Singapore English or Indian English went on to do. Luke and Richards characterised the unique status of English in Hong Kong in the 1980s as an 'auxiliary language', which means 'a non-native language which is reserved for certain restricted functions in society and for use by a restricted section of that society' (Luke and Richards 1982: 55–6). Luke and Richards (1982: 51) thus spoke of the Chinese-speaking and English-speaking populations as two enclosed, socially distant speech communities, with English reserved for 'inter-group' communication.

In the years leading up to the 1997 Handover, Hong Kong was transformed from an industrial centre into a service-oriented economy, which rendered the use of English an indispensable skill in dealing with customers, clients and business partners from all over the world. At the same time, English emerged as an international language and the lingua franca for people whose mother tongues were not English. This put Hong Kong in a unique position, both linguistically and geographically. The introduction of nine years' free education in 1976 had enlarged the population of secondary school students in contact with English; the expansion of tertiary education in the early 1990s further boosted the use of English, since English was the MOI in most universities (the Chinese University being the notable exception) and in most subjects.

The 'instrumental' motivation for learning English has been so great that many Hong Kong students denied that speaking English jeopardised their Chinese identity (Axler et al. 1998; Hyland 1997; Pennington and Yue 1994). The dissociation of English from an English or western culture and identity indicates a first step by which English began to permeate into the social and cultural life of the Hong Kong Chinese. At the same time, a local 'Hong Kong' culture and identity developed in opposition to what was taking place in mainland China. This local culture and identity are symbolised by vernacular Cantonese and Cantonese–English code-switching (Lai 2001), as described in Chapter 5.

6.3 English in the post-colonial era

In 1999, soon after the Handover, Li published an update to Luke and Richards' (1982) study. We have mentioned in Chapter 1 that the situation in Hong Kong now can be described as trilingual and biliterate, and this is how the overall situation is characterised in Li's paper. Whereas Cantonese and English were found to remain important in their respective domains, since Hong Kong had become a Special Administrative Region (SAR) of China the implication was that there would be greater use of Putonghua, and this is indeed what has happened. However, the language situation in Hong Kong was further complicated by the more widespread use of code-mixing or code-switching in spoken conversation and certain print media, a phenomenon which can be seen taken to extremes in Vittachi (2002).

Concerning language use in government, Li (1999) shows that Cantonese had replaced English in press conferences and the Legislative Council as the unmarked language of choice. Court trials could now be conducted in Cantonese, with an interpretation service available, even though English was still used. There was more Chinese in public notices and documents which had previously been written in English. Although many legal ordinances had been translated into Chinese, the original English versions were still the main point of reference, and many cases and precedents are yet to be translated even now.

Reaping the benefits in the advancement of telecommunications, Hong Kong was now seeing more and more English media (for example BBC, CNN, ESPN), and there were also slots for programmes in other languages (Putonghua, Japanese, Korean) which primarily served people speaking these languages as their mother tongues. Despite the availability of different media, Li (1999: 74) believes that the Cantonese-speaking and English-speaking populations remained two 'socially distant', 'enclosed' communities, as there were few media which used both Cantonese and English. Overall, Li (1999: 76) concludes that

Cantonese/Chinese was still dominant in the media, and most ethnic Chinese preferred these media by default, unless for specific purposes like learning English.

In the domain of employment, Li (1999) found that, while the choice and use of language still very much depended on occupation, there were signs that people were using more English in jobs where English was not necessary; this may be due to more contact with westerners as Hong Kong moved to being a service industry. The idea that English was the key to a successful career remained firmly in place, and educational programmes aimed at teaching workplace English had become very popular.

Changes in the education domain had been drastic, and indeed Li (1999) devotes a whole section to the thorny issue of MOI. Hyland (1997: 193) notes that English was the '*de jure* medium of instruction for 91 per cent of secondary school students' before the Handover. This was driven by the perceived socio-economic importance of the language, the belief that English immersion teaching leads to a higher level of English, and also the lack of government support for mother-tongue teaching (So 1992, cited in Hyland 1997: 193). Following the Handover, the government's proposal to change to mother-tongue, that is, Cantonese-medium teaching in secondary schools resulted in allowing only 112 such schools to use English as the MOI, while the remaining 300 schools had to use the mother tongue (Cantonese). This was met with an outcry from parents, students and teachers alike. Although the government's policy to 'uphold mother-tongue teaching and enhance English proficiency concurrently' (Education Commission 2005) is educationally very sound, most parents regard a high level of English proficiency as a guarantee of better career prospects. Thus, the competition for places in the English-medium schools is very high.

Another change, this time at tertiary level, was that there were more universities offering more places to secondary school leavers. All establishments in the tertiary sector which originally taught in English still retain English as their MOI, but even here the picture is not clear-cut. As the student population of Hong Kong is overwhelmingly Cantonese-speaking, and as the majority of university teachers are also Cantonese speakers, it stands to reason that many classes in tertiary institutions are held in Cantonese and not in English. In a survey conducted in one Hong Kong tertiary institution, Balla and Pennington (1996, cited in Pennington 1998a: 3) show that, whereas lectures are usually presented in English, discussions in tutorials are more often in Chinese. A mixture of the two languages is also to be expected. The language policy in tertiary institutions is that classes are held mainly in English, and that students must produce all output for course evaluation in English (unless they are studying another language). The following excerpts from several university websites in Hong Kong illustrate the situation:

> The medium of instruction and assessment at the University is English unless otherwise specified for a particular course or programme. (City University of Hong Kong, http://www.admo.cityu.edu.hk/faq/Home&q=1 023&view=browse&c=776&L=EN&p=1)

> Except for Chinese-related subjects and specially approved programmes, English is used for classes, written assignments and examinations. (Hong Kong Polytechnic University, http://www28.edu.hk//aseprospectus/jsp/misc.jsp?cms_menu_id=5637&websiteId=1&schemeId=200910&langId=1)

> The medium of instruction of the University is English in most cases, although students in the Department of Chinese or the School of Chinese Medicine or taking certain courses offered by the Faculties of Education, Law and Social Sciences may use either Cantonese or Putonghua (Mandarin). All applicants for admission are expected to be fluent in English. Applicants for admission to higher degree studies in Chinese must also be fluent in both written and spoken Chinese. Applicants for admission may be required to sit for English language tests or examinations conducted either by the University or by a public examination authority. (Hong Kong University, http://www.hku.hk/postgrad/intro_medium.htm

> Apart from language courses and courses in the Chinese and Translation Departments, the University uses English mainly as the language of instruction, and this may be supplemented with Cantonese/Putonghua where appropriate. (Lingnan University, http://www.ln.edu.hk/admissions/da/nonjupas/faq.php#04)

> English is the language of instruction HKUST. All applicants must demonstrate their competence in the English language prior to admission. Applicants seeking admission to undergraduate programs with non-local qualifications may satisfy the English language admission requirement through one of the following ways. Other evidence of English proficiency may be considered on individual basis. (Hong Kong University of Science and Technology, http://www.ust.hk/international/admissions/requirements/english.html)

In order to enter university, applicants for all degree-level courses must have grade E (the lowest pass grade) or above in the Hong Kong Advanced Level examination Use of English. Understandably, this gives rise to much discussion – especially in the media – concerning the appropriateness of using English as a requirement for university entrance and as the MOI, particularly when English skills among university applicants are reported to be on the decline. Li (1999) notes that university students and lecturers alike may not be very proficient in English, which may result in the ability of graduates to use English falling short of employers' expectations. However, owing to the drastic socio-political changes in the education system, the average expectation of a graduate's English standard had become much higher, which may disadvantage those whose talent does not lie in English. An additional factor in this may be the pressure to learn Putonghua (Boyle 1999: 33). However, standards are also said to be declining in the subject Chinese Language and Culture at A-level.

In sum, the linguistic situation in Hong Kong had changed since Luke and Richards' (1982) time, from being 'diglossic' to 'polyglossic', with Cantonese, Putonghua and English playing different roles in spoken or written discourse. Li (1999) refers to the situation as 'polyglossia with increasing bilingualism'; different language varieties serve different functions, and more and more people speak English and use it in their daily lives. We may note that perhaps there had already been interplay among three 'languages' back in Luke and Richards' time, but even linguists had been reluctant to recognise that Putonghua and Cantonese were two varieties, rather than dialects under the general heading of 'Chinese'. As for the status of English, Li (1999: 94–5) prefers to use the description 'value added' rather than 'auxiliary' to describe its position, stressing the fact that people see English as key to career opportunities and success even though they can actually live without it in Hong Kong. Li (1999: 96) believes that the concept of English as a 'value added' language was even more popular at a time when the economy in Hong Kong was becoming more service oriented, and more English was used in dealing with customers around the world.

The body of research on language attitudes in Hong Kong converges on the point that, for pragmatic purposes, most Hongkongers aspire to attain an English proficiency level comparable to the standards of British and American English. However, they do not see this aspiration as identifying them with western culture, or dissociating them from Chinese culture. This further illustrates the 'pragmatic' or 'instrumental' motivation behind Hong Kong people learning and using English nowadays. But what is the identity of English in Hong Kong, and how does it affect the identity of its speakers? As reported in Hyland (1997: 202), studies prior to the 1984 Sino-British Joint Declaration on the return of Hong Kong to China showed some hostility to western culture in general and the English language in particular (see, for example, Pierson et al. 1980; Hirvela 1991: 125). However, a more recent publication indicates that, although there had been a growth in Chinese nationalism in Hong Kong since the Handover, it is not in aggressive opposition to the British; rather 'an understandable refocusing on the Chinese roots of Hong Kong's culture' (Boyle 1999: 33). In order to survey Hong Kong tertiary level students' attitude to English, and whether using it compromised their identity to any extent, Hyland (1997) carried out a survey at the time of the Handover. In it, questions relating to the following points were asked (Hyland 1997: 198):

- positive instrumental orientation to English;
- positive orientation to educational and official statuses of English;
- positive affective orientation to English;
- English as not undermining cultural identity;
- English as remaining important in the future.

The results of the survey indicated that, at the time it took place, orientation to English on all of the above points was highly positive, with no indication that respondents felt their cultural identity to be undermined by the use of English (Hyland 1997: 200). In fact, Hyland states:

> for this group of Hong Kongers at least, antipathy and antagonism to English as a local language of colonial power is less significant than recognition of its value as an international language. (Hyland 1997: 207)

He goes on to suggest that the long exposure of the Hong Kong Chinese to English and overseas peoples could lead them to be the best mediators between 'the PRC Chinese and the international business community' (Hyland 1997: 208), something which would seem not to have escaped the international business community or, indeed, the Hong Kong Chinese themselves.

One important finding in recent language surveys (Axler et al. 1998; Pennington and Yue 1994; Hyland 1997) is that 'learners no longer see speaking fluent English as a threat to their Chinese identity'. In our view, this has facilitated the recognition or acceptance of English as an important variety in Hong Kong speakers' linguistic repertoire; and this in turn may lead to the formation of a distinctive Hong Kong variety (see section 6.4).

From the above, it can be seen that English is integrated into Hong Kong life in a way unusual to many other settings in which it is used. This has resulted in a thriving and developing variety of English.

Although there are no, or very few, native speakers of Hong Kong English in the same way as there are native speakers of Singapore English or Indian English, for example, Hong Kong English is an identifiable English, which shows no signs of falling out of use, or becoming merely another learner variety.

Since the publication of Li (1999), the linguistic situation in Hong Kong has continued to move on. In key domains, English has stood up to the challenge presented by the Handover, which had been expected to promote Cantonese, Standard Written Chinese and Putonghua at the expense of English. The need for English has been sustained, if it has not increased, in all sorts of job situations (Evans and Green 2001, 2003), although proficiency in Putonghua is also in high demand. Hong Kong's policy of life-long learning and the encouragement of Hongkongers into postgraduate training further consolidates the position of English as a language of higher education.

One factor in recent years that we think may have been overlooked is the role of 'returnees', that is, Hongkongers who have lived and studied in English-speaking countries such as Britain, Canada, the United States and Australia. Often, they are people who left Hong Kong in the uncertain times before the Handover, and have chosen to return on seeing that the SAR is prospering very much as it was before the end of British sovereignty; equally, they may be the children of parents who were so keen for them to have good English skills that they sent them overseas to school and university. These people can speak English often with a high level of fluency, and we suspect that they will tend to use more English or code-switching with Chinese people. We know of little research specifically looking at this group other than Chen (2008), but would be interested to know how much of an effect returnees are having on the linguistic situation in Hong Kong.

6.4 Hong Kong English: new variety or learner language?

In this section, we will briefly discuss the arguments for and against the existence of a distinctive variety known as Hong Kong English, and how it might develop in the twenty-first century.

This book looks at Hong Kong English as an emergent variety, meaning that it is not as far advanced in its movement towards New Variety status as Singapore or Indian English, but is moving in that direction. It would be negligent, however, not to discuss the issues surrounding this view, as it is by no means universally accepted by those working on English in Hong Kong. Research on features of English in Hong Kong sits firmly in two camps; there is the literature in which it is considered to be a learner interlanguage, such as Chan and Li (2000) and Stibbard (2004), and other works in which it is looked at in terms of being a developing or emergent variety, such as Bolton (2002a) and Hung (2000).

The arguments for and against there being a variety known as Hong Kong English are summarised in Pang (2003). Looking at the argument in favour of the existence of a variety, he draws on two main sources, Bolton (2002b) and Kachru (1982), and evaluates English in Hong Kong in terms of those publications. Bolton, in turn, uses the criteria set down by Butler (1997) in support of his case, which are as follows: (a) a standard and recognisable accent; (b) a distinctive vocabulary to express key features of the physical and social environment; (c) a distinctive history; (d) creative writing, 'written without apology'; and (e) reference works, such as dictionaries.

The first two of Butler's criteria are not in dispute; as demonstrated in this volume as well as elsewhere, English in Hong Kong certainly has a recognisable accent which appears to vary little amongst individual speakers, has a distinctive vocabulary, and also displays distinctive grammatical and discourse features. Concerning the third criterion, Bolton (2002b) points to the lengthy history of linguistic contact between Hong Kong and China and the English, and cites Baker's (1983: 478) assertion that 'Hong Kong Man', a construct which first appeared in the 1960s, 'speaks English or expects his children to'. However, Pang (2003) argues that Hong Kong's colonial past, in which 'good English' was imposed on the population at the onset of British rule, as it was in many territories, means that English in the region developed exonormatively, that is, based on British English. Had it been permitted to develop further endonormatively from the original pidgin which had developed before British colonial rule, there would, in Pang's opinion, be a better case for its being a variety. Concerning the fourth criterion, even though works in Hong Kong English exist, they are somewhat scarce, and Pang (2003: 14) points out that 'they are for international rather than local consumption'. Finally, reference works are scarce. We hope that this book will go some way to resolving that particular problem.

Kachru's (1982) well-known paradigm in the categorisation of varieties and types of English in the world describes three circles: the Inner Circle, the Outer Circle and the Expanding Circle. The Inner Circle includes British and American English, which are said to be 'norm providing', in that these varieties are the ones from which many others have developed, or upon which they are based. The Outer Circle includes Indian and Singapore English, which are described as 'norm developing', meaning that these varieties are developing their own features and standards, and becoming what is sometimes referred to as a 'New Variety of English'. The development here is endonormative, meaning it is not or no longer based on varieties in the Inner Circle, but innovative within the variety itself. This group is often equated with learners or speakers of English as a Second language (ESL), as English is used within the speech community for official purposes (government, education and so on), and may also be used in the home. Expanding Circle Englishes are those for which there is no use for English within the speech community; speakers generally use the language to communicate with 'others'. Members of this group include Japan, Taiwan and mainland China. Those using English in this group are more akin to speakers or learners of English as a Foreign Language (EFL), and are still dependent on the norms of the Inner Circle groups; hence, they are 'norm dependent'. However, we have seen from the discussion above that Hong Kong English does not fit easily into this paradigm, as it is neither a typical Outer Circle English, nor a typical Expanding Circle English.

Within the paradigm of Kachru's three circles (1982), the criteria for a variety to be considered as institutionalised, or belonging to the Outer Circle, are as follows: (a) the length of time in use; (b) the extension of its use; (c) the emotional attachment of second language users to particular varieties; (d) the variety's functional importance; and (e) its sociolinguistic status. Pang (2003: 15) considers (b), (c), (d) and (e) to be 'crucial' to indigenisation, and we feel that we have shown support in this book for all the points except perhaps for (c). Pang, however, points out that, in the case of English in Hong Kong, the fact that it belongs so clearly to certain domains and fields of usage and that it has remained a 'high' variety (Pang 2003: 15), whose development remains based on British and American norms, has hindered its indigenisation. He goes so far as to suggest that the situation will not change so long as teachers of English in Hong Kong and the Hong Kong SAR government cleave to exonormative standards. There are several languages available to the Hongkonger which perform different economic, cultural and social functions, says Pang, and English is limited in its remit and 'remains weak in terms of interpersonal functions' (Pang 2003: 15). Pang concludes that 'English survives in Hong Kong mainly as an acrolect, not serving an integrationist function' (2003: 17).

Perhaps the variety can better be defined in terms of Schneider's Dynamic Model of the Evolution of Postcolonial Englishes (2007). Schneider looks at the socio-political background, identity constructions, sociolinguistic conditions and linguistic effects of each stage in order to arrive at a classification of New Englishes. The model has five phases: foundation, exonormative stabilisation, nativisation, endo-normative stabilisation and differentiation. Foundation (phase 1) can be described as the initial stage at which English is brought to a terri-tory by a 'significant group of settlers' (Schneider 2007: 33), whether by immigration, invasion or occupation. Exonormative stabilisation (phase 2) is the point at which English is regularly used by the settlers as the language of institutions such as government, education and the law, while the settlers still consider themselves to be in an outpost of Britain; the indigenous peoples perceive themselves to be members of a social group which is different from the settlers', but also perceive the advantage of being able to use the settlers' language in terms of socio-economic gain, and become 'English knowing' (Schneider 2007: 39). Inter-racial marriages take place, and children of mixed race are born. Nativisation (phase 3) involves both linguistic and cultural transforma-tion; the intertwining of the old and the new 'is in full swing' (Schneider 2007: 40), and there is a move towards independence from the distant country of origin, politically, linguistically and culturally. Economic independence is gained at this stage, and difference in cultural back-ground and identity is much reduced. Endonormative stabilisation (phase 4) is not achieved until there is political independence, although Schneider notes that this one criterion is sometimes not enough (2007: 48), and that a sense of cultural self-reliance is also required (he gives Australia and New Zealand as examples). In linguistic terms, instead of referring to 'English in X', where 'X' stands for the country, the refer-ence is now to 'X English', where the latter indicates that the English spoken in the territory is a variety in its own right, on equal terms with other varieties. Phase 5, differentiation, is seen as a turning point, a point at which there is no question of the status of the variety, and at which regional and social dialects of that variety begin to assert themselves.

Schneider discusses Hong Kong English in terms of this paradigm, and concludes that 'it can be regarded as having reached phase 3, with some traces of phase 2 still observable' (2007: 133), although, despite its not having reached phase 4, he does use the term 'Hong Kong English' in discussing it. Singapore English, by comparison, has been journeying through phase 4 since the 1970s (Schneider 2007: 155); this is attributed to processes of nation-building (including language policy), modernisa-tion and economic growth which took place post-independence in 1965. With the recent return of Hong Kong to China, Schneider suggests that the development of Hong Kong English will be an interesting test case for the Dynamic Model, but notes that the drive to use English is 'stronger than might have been anticipated' (2007: 139). We have already considered the strength of this drive in the sections above.

There is further light at the end of the tunnel for supporters of Hong Kong English as a New Variety. As mentioned at the end of Chapter 5, Pang explains that 'a change is seeping in with technological applications' (2003: 17), and describes how English and Chinese code-switching is prevalent in email and ICQ interactions amongst Hongkongers, with Cantonese expressions integrated into English sentences rather than the opposite. Four years earlier, Chan's (1999) study looked at Hong Kong English in an internet chat room, and found that either English or Cantonese could be used as the matrix language. This phenomenon, suggests Pang (2003), may eventually lead to the indigenisation of English in Hong Kong. We take his suggestion to mean that Hong Kong English will eventually be pushed more firmly towards Kachru's Outer Circle, Schneider's phase 4, and closer to New Variety status.

Note

1. This publication is available at www.gld.gov.hk/cgi-bin/gld/egazette/index.cgi?lang=e.

7 Annotated bibliography

This chapter starts by surveying general works on Hong Kong English and then goes on to consider specific books and key articles in each area.

7.1 General works on Hong Kong English

Both Platt (1982) and McArthur (2002) provide a comprehensive overview of all the features of Hong Kong English with reference to the larger context of varieties of Asian Englishes, while Kirkpatrick's (2007) description is presented in terms of implications for international communication and pedagogy.

Pennington (1998b) is an edited volume of nineteen chapters, in which authors discuss the linguistic situation in Hong Kong in the run-up to the Handover in 1997, not all of them on Hong Kong English. Wright and Kelly-Holmes (1997) survey the changes in language use during this period.

Kingsley Bolton has published extensively on Hong Kong English. Examples of his work include Bolton (2003), which is a sociolinguistic history of Chinese Englishes, including English in Hong Kong, and Bolton (2002a), which draws together sixteen chapters from different authors on linguistic and literary topics, including information on finding resources for analysing the variety, and ends with a chapter pondering the future for Hong Kong English.

For a historical perspective on language education in Hong Kong, see Lord and Cheng (1987).

7.2 Phonetics and phonology

For a brief overview of some of the features of the phonology of Hong Kong English, see Bolton and Kwok (1990). The first author to attempt a detailed and thorough account of the segmental phonetics and phonology of Hong Kong English in terms of its being an emergent variety is Hung (2000), who, using a quantitative methodology based on word-list data, gives an inventory of phonemes, looks at the phonetic realisation of those phonemes, and suggests distribution of phonemes in the syllable. Acoustic information on voicing and vowel formants is given by Deterding et al. (2008), who also give acoustic measurements of vowels, use connected speech in their description of the variety, and include information on vowel reduction, speech rhythm and sentence stress. Chan and Li (2000) provide an account of the segmental aspects of the English spoken in Hong Kong from the perspective of its being a learner interlanguage. Setter (2008a) discusses the Hong Kong English syllable in depth, and Peng and Setter (2000) look at phonemic alternation in coda consonant clusters. Wong and Setter (2002) consider a possible /n/ and /l/ merger in syllable initial position.

Concerning word and sentence stress, see Hung (2005), Wong (1991, 2004) and Luke (2008). Setter (2006) discusses Hong Kong English speech rhythm. The most comprehensive account of intonation using a discourse intonation framework is to be found in Cheng et al. (2008).

7.3 Morphosyntax

Platt (1982) and McArthur (2002) are similar in that both provide a list of morphosyntactic properties of Hong Kong English illustrated with examples. However, both lists are rather short and appear to be organised in a random manner. Bolton and Nelson (2002) use the HK-ICE corpus to illustrate several easily observable grammatical features found in Hong Kong English. A few studies have examined specific features of Hong Kong English in great detail. Newbrook (1988), for example, has examined the use of relative clauses and relative pronouns in Hong Kong English. Another example is Budge (1989), who has provided a detailed account of the plural marking feature in Hong Kong English. While Gisborne (2000) compares the relative clauses of Hong Kong English with those in Standard English, Lee and Collins (2004) compare the usage of five auxiliary verbs found in Hong Kong English and Australian English.

Other studies mainly employ an error analysis or a contrastive approach to analyse the English produced by Hong Kong Cantonese speakers. For example, Bunton (1989) is a reference book consisting of an alphabetical list of errors produced by Hongkongers. Webster et al. (1987) have analysed the writing produced by Hong Kong secondary students by contrasting Chinese and English. Green (1996) has pointed out that the topic-prominent structure in learners' English is a result of their first language. A. Chan (2004a, 2004b) has used translation tasks to elicit data to illustrate the syntactic transfer from Chinese into English.

7.4 Discourse and lexis

Fung and Carter (2007b) analyse the use of various discourse markers in a corpus of speech produced by Hong Kong students. Cheng and Warren (2001b) focus on the use of *actually* by Hong Kong speakers. Cheng and Warren (2001a) and Wong (2007) discuss the forms and functions of tag questions in Hong Kong English, and they also give an account of their infrequency with reference to non-Hong Kong speakers. Bolton et al. (2002) examine the use of connectors by Hong Kong students in written discourse. Berry (1999/2000) investigates the use of pronouns in Hong Kong newspapers.

Bolton (2003: 209–20) provides a detailed description of Hong Kong English vocabulary, and Benson (2000) argues for its autonomy. Taylor (1989), Carless (1995) and Chow (2001) discuss Hong Kong English vocabulary in Hong Kong newspapers, whereas Chan (1999) analyses Hong Kong English vocabulary on the internet.

7.5 Code-switching

See Gibbons (1987) for an overview of various issues pertaining to Cantonese–English code-mixing in Hong Kong. Luke (1998) distinguishes two types of code-mixing, namely, expedient language mixing and orientational language mixing. Li (2000) discusses the primary motivations of code-switching to English; that is, English is often used in euphemisms, bilingual puns, and expressions whose meaning is more or less specific than their Cantonese counterparts; alternatively, the code-switched expressions are more economical than the pure Cantonese expressions. Lin (1996) is a discussion of code-switching in the classroom, where the forms and functions of code-switching are not quite the same as those in data discussed by Luke (1998) or Li (2000). Chen (2008) is more concerned with variation, and focuses on different code-mixing styles of local Hong Kong bilinguals and 'returnees' respectively.

Moving on to written or media discourse, see Lee (2000), who analyses code-switching in fashion magazines in terms of aesthetic and ideological functions. Fung and Carter (2007a) discuss code-switching in electronic media. Chan (2009) examines code-switching in Cantonese popular songs, and contends that code-switching is very often multi-functional and that the functions of code-switching vary across different genres.

For an account of the morphosyntax of Cantonese–English code-switching in Hong Kong, see Chan (1998a, 1998b) and Leung (2001).

7.6 The history of Hong Kong English

As mentioned above, Bolton (2003) gives a comprehensive socio-historical account of how English in China was used and learnt by Chinese speakers, as well as how English came into contact with Chinese languages or dialects. There are two chapters which are particularly relevant to Hong Kong. Chapter 2 outlines the sociolinguistic situation of late colonial Hong Kong, while chapter 4 charts the emergence of Hong Kong English. Luke and Richards (1982) is an earlier work which describes the use of English in various domains. Some of the descriptions there may sound somewhat outdated – for example, English at the time of the study was spoken only by an elite of Hong Kong people, and the use of English was restricted to largely written communication in the workplace – but presumably the paper reflects the status and functions of English in Hong Kong in the 1970s. See Li (1999) for an update; the picture here is that in the 1990s the use of English was much more pervasive in different domains and across various sectors of the population. Evans and Green (2003) look at the use of English among professionals in Hong Kong, their survey results indicating that English remains important in the employment domain after the 1997 Handover; however, spoken English is seen to be in greater demand in certain sectors and for the higher positions.

There has been a series of language attitude surveys which consistently show that, starting from the 1990s, Hong Kong students (secondary students or university students) have been highly motivated to learn English and do not see speaking fluent English as a betrayal of their Chinese identity. The key works in this area are Pierson et al. (1980), Pennington and Yue (1994), Hyland (1997) and Lai (2001).

There is some discussion in Joseph (2004) and Pang (2003) about the status and future prospects of Hong Kong English. Schneider (2003, 2007) proposes a five-stage model for the development of new Englishes, and considers that Hong Kong English is now undergoing the third developmental stage, referred to as 'nativisation'.

7.7 References

Auer, P. (ed.) (1998), *Code-Switching in Conversation: Language, Interaction and Identity*, London: Routledge.

Axler, M., A. Yang and T. Stevens (1998), 'Current language attitudes of Hong

Kong Chinese adolescents and young adults', in Pennington (1998b), pp. 329–38.

Baker, H. D. (1983), 'Life in the cities: The emergence of Hong Kong man, *China Quarterly* 95: 469–79.

Baker, P. (1987), 'Historical developments in Chinese pidgin English and the nature of the relationships between the various pidgin Englishes of the Pacific region', *Journal of Pidgin and Creole Languages* 2: 163–207.

Baker, P. and P. Mühlhäusler (1990), 'From business to pidgin', *Journal of Asian-Pacific Communication* 1: 87–115.

Balla, J. and M. C. Pennington (1996), 'The perception of English-medium instruction by tertiary-level vocational students in Hong Kong', *Education Journal* 24: 131–54.

Bauer, L. (1983), *English Word-Formation*, Cambridge: Cambridge University Press.

Bauer, R. S. (1982), 'Cantonese sociolinguistic patterns: correlating social characteristics of speakers with phonological variables in Hong Kong Cantonese', unpublished PhD thesis, University of California.

Bauer, R. S. and P. K. Benedict (eds) (1997), *Modern Cantonese Phonology*, Berlin and New York: Mouton de Gruyter.

Bauer, R. S. and C. S. P. Wong (2008), 'ABC etymological dictionary of English loanwords in Hong Kong Cantonese', unpublished manuscript.

Benson, P. (2000), 'Hong Kong words: variation and context', *World Englishes* 19(3): 373–80.

Benson, P. (2002), 'Hong Kong words: variation and context', in Bolton (2002a), pp. 161–70.

Berry, R. (1999/2000), 'We in Hong Kong: Claiming to speak for the community', *Asian Englishes* 2(2): 5–25.

Bolton, K. (ed.) (2002a), *Hong Kong English: Autonomy and Creativity*, Hong Kong: Hong Kong University Press.

Bolton, K. (2002b), 'The sociolinguistics of Hong Kong and the space for Hong Kong English', in Bolton (2002a), pp. 29–55.

Bolton, K. (2003), *Chinese Englishes: A Sociolinguistic History*, Cambridge: Cambridge University Press.

Bolton, K. and H. Kwok (1990), 'The dynamics of the Hong Kong accent: social identity and sociolinguistic description', *Journal of Asian Pacific Communication* 1(1): 147–72.

Bolton, K. and G. Nelson (2002), 'Analysing Hong Kong English: sample texts from the International Corpus of English', in Bolton (2002a), pp. 241–62.

Bolton, K., G. Nelson and J. Hung (2002), 'A corpus-based study of connectors in student writing: research from the International Corpus of English in Hong Kong (ICE-HK)', *International Journal of Corpus Linguistics* 7(2): 165–82.

Boyle, J. (1999), 'International intelligibility and teaching English pronunciation in Hong Kong', *Speak Out!* 24: 33–9.

Bradford, B. (1997), 'Upspeak in British English', *English Today* 51(13.3): 29–36.

Bradshaw, J. (1997), 'Phonological change in progess in a second language? A preliminary analysis of variation in the usage of a speaker of Hong Kong English', Hong Kong Polytechnic University *Working Papers in ELT and Applied Linguistics* 2(2): 21–36.

Brown, A. (1988), 'The staccato effect in the pronunciation of English in Malaysia and Singapore', in J. Foley (ed.), *New Englishes: The Case of Singapore*, Singapore: Singapore University Press, pp. 115–47.

Brown, P. and S. Levinson (1987), *Politeness: Some Universals in Language Usage*, Cambridge: Cambridge University Press.

Budge, C. (1989), 'Plural marking in Hong Kong English', *Hong Kong Papers in Linguistics and Language Teaching* 12: 39–47.

Bunton, D. (1989), *Common English Errors in Hong Kong*, Hong Kong: Longman Hong Kong Education.

Butler, S. (1997), 'Corpus of English in South East Asia: implications for a regional dictionary', in M. L. S. Bautista (ed.), *English as an Asian Language: The Philippine Context*, Manila: Macquarie Library, pp. 103–24.

Carless, D. (1995), 'Political expressions in the *South China Morning Post*', *English Today* 42: 18–22.

Chan, A. Y. W. (2004a), 'Syntactic transfer: evidence from the interlanguage of Hong Kong Chinese ESL learners', *Modern Language Journal* 88(1): 56–74.

Chan, A. Y. W. (2004b), '*The boy who Mary loves him is called John*: a study of the resumptive pronoun problem and its correction strategies', *Hong Kong Journal of Applied Linguistics* 9(1): 53–69.

Chan, A. Y. W. (2006), 'Strategies used by Cantonese speakers in pronouncing English initial consonant clusters: insights into the interlanguage phonology of Cantonese ESL learners in Hong Kong', *International Review of Applied Linguistics in Language Teaching* 44(4): 331–55.

Chan, A. Y. W. and D. C. S. Li (2000), 'English and Cantonese phonology in contrast: explaining Cantonese ESL learners' English pronunciation problems', *Language, Culture and Curriculum* 13(1): 67–85.

Chan, B. H. S. (1992), 'Code-mixing in Hong Kong Cantonese–English bilinguals: constraints and processes', unpublished MA dissertation, Department of English, Chinese University of Hong Kong.

Chan, B. H. S. (1998a), 'How does Cantonese–English code-mixing work?', in Pennington (1998b), pp. 191–216.

Chan, B. H. S. (1998b), 'Functional heads, Cantonese phrase structure and Cantonese-English code-switching', *UCL Working Papers in Linguistics* 10: 254–84.

Chan, B. H. S. (2003), *Aspects of the Syntax, the Pragmatics and the Production of Code-Switching: Cantonese and English*, New York: Peter Lang.

Chan, B. H. S. (2004), 'Case-marking in Cantonese–English code-switching', *Proceedings of XVII International Congress of Linguists, Session 2: Pidgins, Creoles and Languages in Contact*, CD-ROM included in P. Van Sterkenburg (ed.), *Linguistics Today: Facing a Greater Challenge*, Amsterdam: John Benjamins.

Chan, B. H. S. (2009), 'English in Hong Kong Cantopop', *World Englishes* (28)1: 107–129.

Chan', M. and H. Kwok (1982), *A Study of Lexical Borrowing from English in Hong Kong Chinese*, Hong Kong: Centre of Asian Studies, University of Hong Kong.

Chan, M. and H. Kwok (1985), *A Study of Lexical Borrowing from Chinese into English with Special Reference to Hong Kong*, Hong Kong: Centre of Asian Studies, University of Hong Kong.

Chan, V. H. F. (1999), 'Hong Kong English and the internet', unpublished MA dissertation, University of Hong Kong.

Chao, Y. R. (1947), *Cantonese Primer*, Cambridge, MA: Harvard University Press.

Chen, K. H. Y. (2008), 'Positioning and repositioning: linguistic practices and identity negotiation of overseas returning bilinguals in Hong Kong', *Multilingua* 27(1/2): 57–75.

Cheng, H. N. and R. N. Zi (1987), 'In-house English language training: a survey of 15 organisations', in R. Lord and H. N. Cheng (eds), *Language Education in Hong Kong*, Hong Kong: Chinese University Press, pp. 173–85.

Cheng, N. L., K. C. Shek, K. K. Tse and S. L. Wong (1973), *At What Cost? Instruction through the English Medium in Hong Kong Schools*, Hong Kong: Shum Shing.

Cheng, W. and M. Warren (2001a), 'She knows about Hong Kong than you do isn't it? Tags in Hong Kong conversational English', *Journal of Pragmatics* 33(9): 1419–39.

Cheng, W. and M. Warren (2001b), 'The functions of *actually* in a corpus of intercultural conversations', *International Journal of Corpus Linguistics* 6(2): 257–80.

Cheng, W., C. Greaves and M. Warren (2008), *A Corpus-Driven Study of Discourse Intonation*, Amsterdam and Philadelphia: John Benjamins.

Cheung, H-N. S. (1972), *Cantonese as Spoken in Hong Kong*, Hong Kong: Chinese University of Hong Kong. [In Chinese]

Cheung, K. H. (1986), 'The Phonology of Present Day Cantonese', unpublished PhD thesis, University College London.

Cho, T. and P. Ladefoged (1999), 'Variation and universals in VOT: evidence from 18 languages', *Journal of Phonetics* 27: 207–29.

Chow, S. P. M. (2001), 'The study of Hong Kong English vocabulary with particular reference to the study of official and political discourse in the HKSAR', unpublished MA dissertation, University of Hong Kong.

Cowles, R. T. (1965), '*The Cantonese Speaker's Dictionary,* Hong Kong: Hong Kong University Press.

Cruttenden, A. (1997), '*Intonation,* (2nd edn), Cambridge: Cambridge University Press.

Cruttenden, A. (ed.) (2008), *Gimson's Pronunciation of English,* (7th edn), London: Arnold.

Cummings, P. J. (2007), 'A study of lexical innovations in Hong Kong English', unpublished MA dissertation, University of Hong Kong.

Dauer, R. M. (1983), 'Stress timing and syllable timing reanalyzed', *Journal of Phonetics* 11: 51–62.

Deterding, D. (2007), *Singapore English*, Edinburgh: Edinburgh University Press.

Deterding, D., J. Wong and A. Kirkpatrick (2008), 'The pronunciation of Hong Kong English', *English World-Wide* 29(2): 148–75.

Evans, S. and C. Green (2001), 'Language in post-colonial Hong Kong: the roles of English and Chinese in the public and private sectors', *English World-Wide* 22: 247–58.

Evans, S. and C. Green (2003), 'The use of English by Chinese professionals in post-1997 Hong Kong', *Journal of Multilingual and Multicultural Development* 24(5): 386–412.

Fung, L. and R. Carter (2007a), 'Cantonese e-discourse: a new hybrid variety of English', *Multilingua* 26: 35–66.

Fung, L. and R. Carter (2007b), 'Discourse markers and spoken English: Native and learner use in pedagogic settings', *Applied Linguistics* 28(3): 410–39.

Gardner-Chloros, P. (2009), *Code-Switching*, Cambridge: Cambridge University Press.

Gibbons, J. (1979), 'U-gay-wa: a linguistic study of the campus language of students at the university of Hong Kong', in R. Lord (ed.), *Hong Kong Language Papers*, Hong Kong: Hong Kong University Press, pp. 3–43.

Gibbons, J. (1987), *Code-Mixing and Code-Choice: A Hong Kong Case Study*, Clevedon: Multilingual Matters.

Gisborne, N. (2000), 'Relative clauses in Hong Kong English', *World Englishes* 19(3): 357–71.

Green, C. (1996), 'The origins and effects of topic-prominence in Chinese–English interlanguage', *International Review of Applied Linguistics* 34(2): 119–34.

Grosjean, F. (1982), *Life with Two Languages: An Introduction to Bilingualism*, Cambridge, MA: Harvard University Press.

Gumperz, J. J. (1982), *Discourse Strategies*, Cambridge: Cambridge University Press.

Heller, M. (ed.) (1988), *Codeswitching: Anthropological and Sociolinguistic Perspectives*, Berlin: Mouton de Gruyter.

Hirvela, A. (1991), 'Footing the English bill in Hong Kong: language politics and linguistic schizophrenia', *Journal of Asian Pacific Communication* 2(1): 117–37.

Ho, J. W. Y. (2006), 'Functional complementarity between two languages in ICQ', *International Journal of Bilingualism* 10(4): 429–51.

Huddleston, R. and G. Pullum (2002), *The Cambridge Grammar of the English Language*, Cambridge: Cambridge University Press.

Hung, T. (2000), 'Towards a phonology of Hong Kong English', *World Englishes* 19(3): 337–56.

Hung, T. (2005), 'Word stress in Hong Kong English: a preliminary study', *Hong Kong Baptist University Papers in Applied Language Studies* 9: 29–40.

Hyland, K. (1997), 'Language attitudes at the Handover: communication and identity in Hong Kong', *English World-Wide* 18(2): 191–210.

Jenkins, J. (2000), *The Phonology of English as an International Language*, Oxford: Oxford University Press.

Johnson, R. K. (1983), 'Bilingual switching strategies: a study of the modes of teacher-talk in bilingual secondary classrooms in Hong Kong', *Language Learning and Communication* 2: 267–85.

Joseph, J. E. (2004), *Language and Idenity: National, Ethnic, Religious*, Basingstoke: Palgrave Macmillan.

Kachru, B. B. (1982), *The Other Tongue: English Across Cultures*, Oxford: Pergamon Press.

Kachru, B. B. (2005), *Asian English: Beyond the Canon*, Hong Kong: Hong Kong University Press.

Kachru, Y. and C. L. Nelson (2006), *World Englishes in an Asian Context*, Hong Kong: Hong Kong University Press.

Kirkpatrick, A. (2007), *World Englishes: Implications for International Communication and English Language Teaching*, Cambridge: Cambridge University Press.

Kiu, K. L. (1977), 'Tonal rules for English loan words in Cantonese', *Journal of the International Phonetic Association* 7(1): 17–22.

Lai, M. L. (2001), 'Hong Kong students' attitudes towards Cantonese', Putonghua and English after the change of sovereignty', *Journal of Multilingual and Multicultural Development* 22(2): 112–33.

Lai, R. Y. K. (2006), 'Language mixing in an English-Cantonese child with uneven development', unpublished MPhil thesis, The University of Hong Kong. (Downloaded from http://library.hku.hk)

Lee, C. K.M. (2007), 'Linguistic features of email and ICQ instant messaging in Hong Kong', in B. Danet and S. C. Herring (eds.), *The Multilingual Internet: Language, Communication and Culture Online*, New York: Oxford University Press, pp. 184–208.

Lee, J. F. K. and P. Collins (2004), 'On the usage of *have, dare, need, ought* and *used to* in Australian English and Hong Kong English', *World Englishes* 23(4): 501–13.

Lee, M. P. Y. (2000), 'Code-switching in media texts: its implications on society and culture in post-colonial Hong Kong', in D. C. S. Li, A. M. Y. Lin and W. K. Tsang (eds), *Language and Education in Post-Colonial Hong Kong*, Hong Kong: Linguistic Society of Hong Kong, pp. 95–130.

Leung, Y. B. (1987), 'Constraints on intrasentential code-mixing in Cantonese and English', unpublished M.A. dissertation, University of Hong Kong.

Leung, T. C. (2001), 'An optimality-theoretic approach to Cantonese/English code-switching', unpublished MPhil dissertation, The University of Hong Kong.

Li, D. C. S. (1996), *Issues in Bilingualism and Biculturalism: A Hong Kong Case Study*, New York: Peter Lang.

Li, D. C. S. (1998), 'The plight of the purist', in Pennington (1998b), pp. 161–90.

Li, D. C. S. (1999), 'The functions and status of English in Hong Kong: A post-1997 update', *English World-Wide* 20(1): 61–110.

Li, D. C. S. (2000), 'Cantonese–English code-switching research in Hong Kong: a Y2K review', *World Englishes* 19(3): 305–22.

Li, D. C. S. (2001), 'L2 lexis in L1: reluctance to translate out of concern for referential meaning', *Multilingua* 20(1): 1–26.

Li, D. C. S. and E. C. Y. Tse (2002), 'One day in the life of a "purist"', *International Journal of Bilingualism* 6(2): 147–202.

Lin, A. M. Y. (1996), 'Bilingualism or linguistic segregation? Symbolic domination, resistance and code switching in Hong Kong schools', *Linguistics and Education* 8: 49–84.

Lin, I. (2008), 'Questions and responses in business communication in Hong Kong', unpublished PhD dissertation, Hong Kong Polytechnic University.

Linguistic Society of Hong Kong (1997), *Cantonese Romanization Scheme*, Hong Kong: Linguistic Society of Hong Kong. [In Chinese]

Liu, J., E. Tindall and D. Nisbet (2006), 'Chinese learners and English plural forms', *Linguistics Journal* 1(3): 127–47.

Lock, G. (2003), 'Being international, local and Chinese: advertisements on the Hong Kong mass transit railway', *Visual Communication* 2: 195–214.

Lord, R. and H. N. L. Cheng (1987), *Language Education in Hong Kong*, Hong Kong: The Chinese University Press.

Low, E. L., E. Grabe and F. Nolan (2000), 'Quantitative characterisations of speech rhythm: syllable-timing in Singapore English', *Language and Speech* 43(4): 377–401.

Luke, K. K. (1998), 'Why two languages might be better than one: motivations of language mixing in Hong Kong', in Pennington (1998b), pp. 145–60.

Luke, K. K. (2008), 'Stress and intonation in Hong Kong English', paper given at the 14th International Association of World Englishes conference, City University, Hong Kong, December.

Luke, K. K. and J. C. Richards (1982), 'English in Hong Kong: functions and status', *English World-Wide* 3: 47–64.

Matthews, S. and V. Yip (1994), *Cantonese: A Comprehensive Grammar*, London and New York: Routledge.

McArthur, T. (2002), *The Oxford Guide to World English*, Oxford: Oxford University Press.

Milroy, L. and P. Muysken (eds) (1995), *One Speaker, Two Languages: Cross-Disciplinary Perspectives on Code-switching*, Cambridge: Cambridge University Press.

Morrison, K. and I. Liu (2000), 'Ideology, linguistic capital, and the medium of instruction in Hong Kong', *Journal of Multilingual and Multicultural Development* 21(6): 471–86.

Morrison, R. D. D. (1828), *A Vocabulary of the Canton Dialect*, Macao: East India Company.

Myers-Scotton, C. (1993a), *Social Motivations for Codeswitching: Evidence from Africa*, New York: Oxford University Press.

Myers-Scotton, C. (1993b), *Duelling Languages: Grammatical Structure in Codeswitching*, Oxford: Clarendon Press.

Myers-Scotton, C. (2002), *Contact Linguistics: Bilingual Encounters and their Grammatical Outcomes*, Oxford: Oxford University Press.

Newbrook, M. (1988), 'Relative clauses, relative pronouns and Hong Kong English', *University of Hong Kong Papers on Linguistics and Language Teaching* 11: 25–41.

Pang, T. T. T. (2003), 'Hong Kong English: A stillborn variety?', *English Today* 74(19/2): 12–18.

Peng, L. and J. Setter (2000), 'The emergence of systematicity in the English pronunciations of two Cantonese-speaking adults in Hong Kong', *English World-Wide* 21(1): 81–108.

Pennington, M. C. (1998a), 'Colonialism's aftermath in Asia: a snapshot view of bilingualism in Hong Kong', *Hong Kong Journal of Applied Linguistics* 3(1): 1–16.

Pennington, M. C. (ed.) (1998b), *Language in Hong Kong at Century's End*, Hong Kong: Hong Kong University Press.

Pennington, M. C. and F. Yue (1994), 'English and Chinese in Hong Kong: pre-1997 language attitudes', *World Englishes* 13(1): 1–20.

Pierson, H., G. S. Fu and S. Y. Lee (1980), 'An analysis of the relationship between language attitudes and English attainment of secondary school students in Hong Kong', *Language Learning* 30: 289–316.

Platt, J. T. (1982), 'English in Singapore, Malaysia, and Hong Kong', in R. W. Bailey and M. Gorlach (eds), *English as a World Language*, Cambridge: Cambridge University Press, pp. 384–414.

Przedlacka, J. (2002), *Estuary English? A Sociophonetic Study of Teenage Speech in the Home Counties*, Frankfurt, Berlin, Bern, Brussells, New York and Oxford: Peter Lang.

Radio Television Hong Kong (2006), *The Story of Hong Kong: Talking about Cantonese*, Hong Kong: Radio Television Hong Kong. [Television programme]

Reynolds, S. (1985), 'Code-switching in Hong Kong', unpublished M.A. dissertation, University of Hong Kong.

Roach, P. (1982), 'On the distinction between "stress-timed" and "syllable-timed" languages', in D. Crystal (ed.), *Linguistic Controversies: Essays in Linguistic Theory and Practice in Honour of F. R. Palmer*, London: Arnold, pp. 73–9.

Roach, P. (2009), *English Phonetics and Phonology: A Practical Course*, (4th edn), Cambridge: Cambridge University Press.

Romaine, S. (1995), *Bilingualism*, (2nd edn), Oxford: Blackwell.

Rosewarne, D. (1984), 'Estuary English', *Times Educational Supplement*, 19 October.

Rosewarne, D. (1994a), 'Estuary English – tomorrow's RP?', *English Today* 10(1): 3–8.

Rosewarne, D. (1994b), 'Pronouncing Estuary English', *English Today* 10(4): 3–7.

Schiffrin, D. (1987), *Discourse Markers*, Cambridge: Cambridge University Press.

Schneider, E. (2003), 'The dynamics of new Englishes: from identity construction to dialect birth', *Language* 79(2): 233–81.

Schneider, E. W. (2007), *Postcolonial English: Varieties Around the World*, Cambridge: Cambridge University Press.

Scollon, R. (1993), 'Culminative ambiguity: conjunctions in Chinese–English intercultural communication', *Working Papers of the Department of English*, Hong Kong: City Polytechnic of Hong Kong, pp. 55–73.

Scollon, R. and S. Scollon (2000), *Intercultural Communication: A Discourse Approach* (2nd edn), Oxford: Blackwell.

Setter, J. (2006), 'Speech rhythm in World Englishes: the case of Hong Kong', *TESOL Quarterly* 40(4): 763–82.

Setter, J. (2008a), 'Consonant clusters in Hong Kong English', *World Englishes* 27(3/4): 502–15.

Setter, J. (2008b), 'Prosody in Hong Kong English: aspects of speech rhythm and intonation', paper given at the 14th International Association of World Englishes conference, City University, Hong Kong, December.

Setter, J. and D. Deterding (2003), 'Extra final consonants in the English of Hong Kong and Singapore', *Proceedings of the 15th International Congress of Phonetic Sciences*, Barcelona, August: 1875–8.

Shi, D.-X. (1991), 'Chinese Pidgin English: its origin and linguistic features', *Journal of Chinese Linguistics* 19: 1–40.

Singh, I. (2001), *Pidgins and Creoles*, London: Arnold.

So, D. (1992), 'Language-based bifurcation of secondary education in Hong Kong', in K. K. Luke (ed.), *Issues in Language Education in Hong Kong*, Hong Kong: Linguistic Society of Hong Kong, pp. 69–96.

Stibbard, R. (2004), 'The spoken English of Hong Kong: a study of co-occurring segmental errors', *Language, Culture and Curriculum* 17(2): 127–42.

Taylor, A. (1989), 'Hong Kong's English newspapers', *English Today* 20: 18–24.

Todd, L. (1990), *Pidgins and Creoles*, (2nd edn), London: Routledge.

Tottie, G. and S. Hoffman (2006), 'Tag questions in British and American English', *Journal of English Linguistics* 34(4): 283–311.

Tsang, W. K. and M. Wong (2004), 'Constructing a shared "Hong Kong identity" in comic discourses', *Discourse & Society* 15(6): 765–85.

Vittachi, N. (2002), 'From Yinglish to sado-mastication', in Bolton (2002a), pp. 207–18.

Walton, A. R. (1983), *Tone, Segment and Syllable in Chinese: A Polydimensional Approach to Surface Phonetic Structure*, Cornell University East Asia Papers No. 32, Cornell University.

Webster, M., A. Ward and K. Craig (1987), 'Language errors due to first language interference (Cantonese) produced by Hong Kong students of English', *Institute of Language in Education Journal* 3: 63–81.

Wells, J. C. (1982), *Accents of English* (3 vols), Cambridge: Cambridge University Press.

Wells, J. C. (2006), *English Intonation*, Cambridge: Cambridge University Press.

Williams, S. W. (1836), 'Jargon spoken at Canton', *Chinese Repository* 4 (January): 428–35.

Wong, C. S. P. (1991), 'The stress patterns of nonsense English words of Cantonese–speaking ESL learners', *Chinese University of Hong Kong Papers in Linguistics* 3: 83–111.

Wong, C. S. P. (2004), 'Does Cantonese lexical tone affect the acquisition of English word stress?', *Proceedings of the Applied Linguistics Association of Korea's 2004 Annual International Conference and General Meeting*, Hanyang University, Korea, December: 193–8.

Wong, C. S. P. and J. Setter (2002), 'Is it "night" or "light"? How and why Cantonese-speaking ESL learners confuse syllable-initial [n] and [l]', in A. James and J. Leather (eds), *New Sounds 2000: Proceedings of the Fourth International Symposium on the Acquisition of Second-Language Speech*, University of Klagenfurt, Austria, pp. 315–59.

Wong, C. S. P., R. S. Bauer and Z. W. M. Lam (2009), 'The integration of English loanwords in Hong Kong Cantonese', *Journal of the Southeast Asian Linguistics Society* 1: 251–65.

Wong, M. L. Y. (2007), 'Tag questions in Hong Kong English: a corpus-based English', *Asian Englishes* 10(1): 44–61.

Wright, S. and H. Kelly-Holmes (1997), *One Country, Two Systems, Three Languages*, Clevedon: Multilingual Matters.

Yau, M. S. (1993), 'Functions of the two codes in Hong Kong Chinese', *World Englishes* 12(1): 25–33.

Yip, V. (1995), *Interlanguage and Learnability: from Chinese to English*, Amsterdam and Philadelphia: John Benjamins.

Yip, V. and S. Matthews (2007), *The Bilingual Child: Early Development and Language Contact*, Cambridge: Cambridge University Press.

Yiu, E. S. M. (2005), 'Language mixing and grammatical development in a Cantonese-English balanced bilingual child in Hong Kong', unpublished MPhil thesis, The University of Hong Kong.

Yule, G. (2003), '*The Study of Language* (3rd edn), Cambridge: Cambridge University Press.

Zee, E. (1996), 'Phonological changes in Hong Kong Cantonese', *Current Issues in Language and Society* 3: 192–200.

8 Transcripts for the data from our speakers

8.1 Transcription conventions

Int	the speech of the interviewer
01/05/08/09/10	the speech of the interviewee
HE	the 'happy event' recording
MT	the 'map task' recording
60	shown in the left-hand column: the time reached during a line of dialogue from the start of the file (in seconds)
((laughs))	non-linguistic sound
. . .	pause
s–	incomplete word

The interviewer in these recordings is Alois Heuboeck. The first draft of the transcripts was completed by Iran M. Heuboeck.

8.2 Speaker 1: Happy event task (01-HE)

01	when I was a kid erm around the age of erm ten
Int	ten years
01	eleven around and mmm I actually studied and aah in the same primary school with my brother
Int	mhm
01	and the last day before we have our Christmas holiday
Int	okay
01	my dad usually drive his car and pick me up
Int	yeah
01	and to take us to Toys R Us – you know the toy store
Int	uhuh
01	and we usually we get our Christmas gifts over there . . . and erm ((tuts)) . . . it's it's quite happy it's not about the the the the gift
Int	yeah

130

01 but instead it's like erm . . . those kind of I k- I I was just being you know so fascinated about you know . . . to to be a kid again I'll say you know in a way like compared to now

Int yes

01 and aah and I remember erm we we spend like hours inside just
60 to find that something we really like you know

Int okay

01 and I use

Int so just your dad and your brother and you

01 yeah cause my mom still have to work at

Int uhuh

01 somewhere else so yeah he drove us there and then we we spent hours over there and pick something we like and usually I discuss with my brother and like aah you ((cough cough)) how about you get this and I get that one and so we can you know play together

Int uhuh

01 you know share it and . . . yeah and we also . . . spend some time getting some kind of aah decorations

Int Christmas

01 decorations

Int yes

01 for our house and . . . ((tsss)) cause we usually we have a Christmas tree of course a fake one an artificial one and erm during Christmas we spend half day decorating the house and the tree as well

Int yeah yeah yes

01 so every year we get something new from Toys R Us

Int uhuh uhuh

01 we got something new decorations Christmas decorations . . . and after that aah we will go to Kentucky Fried Chicken which
120 is right next to it because kids love fries and fried pan-fried stuff and so yeah my dad would take us there and we eat some kind of snacks you know before we go back home for dinner I would say

Int yeah

01 and after we . . . we you know decorate our house the flat I'll say and um ((tss)) and we'll put the gifts right beneath the ((tss)) the tree

Int Yeah

01 and it seems to be you know quite er tempting you know for us to to go open them sometimes you know

Int   uhuh

01   right before you know cause er our rules is 'don't open any gifts before

Int   yeah yeah

01   Boxing Day' and aah

Int   before Boxing Day oh

01   yeah so . . . so yeah so it's like um ((tss))

Int   so the gifts stay eh under the Christmas tree for two days or something like that

01   yeah . . . so

Int   you can see them

01   and we can we we could touch it but we cannot open it

Int   ((laughs))

180 01 so it's it's pretty tempting and um and yeah that's that's like a really happy memory I have during childhood I would say

Int   yeah yeah

01   Yes

Int   so was that the particular Christmas where that was particularly happy or was it er . . . that every year it's happened like this

01   um . . . it we haven't been doing that for quite a few years really cause you know I'm already twenty-one and um . . . er I think that it it's so meaningful or

Int   yeah yeah

01   so happy was er er cause we had exams after right after the Christmas

Int   yeah yeah

01   and . . . and it's it's like a little bit of joy sweetness you know over over that er entire Christmas period cause we spend loads of time in studying cause my mum will will stay at home you know and and you know teach us and and you know force us to study I would say in a way and er so it's like a little bit of sweetness
240   I'll say you know comparing to the entire Christmas process you know cause yeah and like you know in Reading we can we have Christmas holiday with maybe maximum one to two assignments but no exams so you know we still have our private time and

Int   yes yes

01   doing things . . . and yeah so I'll say that's the happiest part I have

Int   that was very nice yeah did you do you remember the gifts you chose for yourself and what your brother had?

01   um ... when I was smaller or around um ... six to seven years old we usually buy Legos

Int   uhuh yeah

01   Legos and er when we get to the age of er ten eleven we start to get the TV games you know

Int   okay

01   Playstation things like these but still yeah I sometimes I I get Legos too so but yeah but not quite often than comparing to ... to ... a few years ago say like when I was six to seven

Int   so you enjoyed playing with Legos at that time

300   01   yeah last week I went to London I actually I wanna I wanna you know play that with the kids you know around me but it but it seems you know it's I have pass the the age of

Int   yes ((laughs))

01   that's the sad part I'll say you know cause we went to London and there's like loads of um kids inside and they got Legos and other kind of things and I was like so you know so tempting for you to to touch those

Int   yes

01   racks of things ... yeah yeah ... that's why it's memorable I'll say

Int   yeah

01   yeah

8.3 Speaker 1: Map task (01-MT)

01   so um I guess you might be able to see there's a diamond mine on your east direction

Int   yes I see that there's a diamond mine yes

01   and you actually go south you know erm I should say on on a parallel direction you know on so you just go south

Int   yes ok

01   and um go round ... the diamond mine

Int   ok um which side do I go round the diamond mine

01   er you should go um let me see ...

Int   say left or right or or

01   you should go left

Int   that's it

01   should go left

Int   ok

01   and walk straight ahead or ((whispering)) walk straight ahead

Int   mhm

60 01   and you might probably be able to see a springboks

    Int   no I don't see a springboks no . . . would that be be where would that be in relation to the diamond mine

    01   it should be on its left its right no on its right I'm sorry

    Int   on the right ok in the east

    01   yeah I'm sorry my left

    Int   east side yes east of the diamond mine

    01   yes and erm after you have reached springboks ((tuts)) um you should um . . . turn left

    Int   right I don't see that so the springboks is that where the highest view point is

    01   er

    Int   springboks

    01   springboks should be . . . on the highest view point . . . left

    Int   on the left ok I can see yeah

    01   ok

    Int   so it's between the two

    01   yeah so there's actually a path between those two

120 Int   right yeah so I go up north

    01   and

    Int   and past the highest view point

    01   and then you go south . . . ahead straight

    Int   ok

    01   and you should be able to see a safari truck

    Int   ok yes there's a safari truck yes

    01   ok and um . . .

    Int   so where do I go in relation to the safari truck

    01   and you should go right it's not entirely right but it's like um ((tuts)) south west direction

    Int   oh south west ok yeah yeah

    01   ok af-

    Int   so I pass west of the safari truck

    01   yes and then you head straight again which is head west

    Int   and then west again yes

    01   yeah and then you should be able to see a field station sorry . . . ((mobile phone rings)) I'm sorry . . . and after

180 Int   I can I can see a field station but that's quite a long way to go . . . that's that's on the other direction on the other side of the map already

    01   ((whispers)) it's on the other side of the map oh right there's actually two field stations

Int oh ok

01 and so

Int I've just got one on here

01 you should go back to um ... ((whispers)) so now you are on

Int I'm south west of the safari truck

01 south west of the safari truck might well be here and ... mmm ... can you see a oh sorry can you see a banana tree on your left

Int yeah I see the banana tree yeah

01 so you have to go round the banana tree on its left or I should say
240 um you should turn left is it or you should go south I should say go south

Int south and which side of the banana tree

01 it should be on the

Int before or after so on the east side or the west side

01 after the banana tree I'm sorry after

Int so on the west side of the banana tree ok yes

01 west side

Int so I go south there

01 yes and then

Int to where do I go now

01 and do you see a gold mine

Int no I see a rock fall but I don't see a gold mine

01 rock fall it's er it's it's ... too far I would say um

Int too far south

01 er yeah too far south I would say erm ... it might be let's see ... um ... can I actually um estimate you know the time frame and to give you directions

Int oh yeah I mean if you say the banana tree and the rock fall you
300 can say half way or you know a third of the way or things like that yeah sure

01 yeah sure ah

Int cause we don't know how much time it would take me any way

01 right

Int to get from the banana tree to the

01 um ... by the er I should say you should you should um now currently you're at the rock fall correct so you should

Int no I'm still at the banana tree

01 you're still at the

Int ok

01 ok or I can say you're at the rock fall ok er if and um ... um I

            should say um you should erm . . . you're currently at the banana tree you should head south

Int   mhm

01   and um you should turn . . . left by the time turn west turn east I should say turn east by the time you . . . it's m- how d'you say

360   er turn left . . . mmm turn left . . . you should turn left according ((whispers)) you should turn left half way through between rock fall and banana tree I say I say

Int   ok that's about the height of the rope bridge isn't it where the rope bridge is there right

01   yes actually you should go through the rope bridge and then . . . turn south again

Int   ok so I walk down the banana tree then turn left towards the east and walk straight to the rope bridge

01   correct

Int   and after that I turn south where the crocodiles are is that right

01   ah . . . crocodiles there's no crocodiles on my map

Int   oh ok yeah

01   but um . . . do you see any giraffes

Int   yes I do yeah they're the crocodiles are north of the giraffes between the rope bridge and the

420   01   ok so you should head towards the giraffe

Int   ok good

01   that means go south

Int   yeah

01   and then you . . . go round the giraffes again which is turning er heading to the west direction

Int   to the west again so is that north or south of the giraffes

01   it should be the south part of the giraffes

Int   south ok so giraffes toward the west again

01   and can you see a great lake

Int   er yes there is a great lake

01   and you should head towards the great lake

Int   ok

01   and you go round again . . . and

Int   great lake

01   yeah so you go south go south of the great lake

Int   oh I have to go south of the great lake ok yes

01   and then um you might have to go north right after it

Int   after the great lake

01   you go

Int   I go
01   north
Int   ok
01   and
Int   toward the rock fall

01   er the rock fall is a little bit too far but er it's um ... ((tuts)) it's it's
480   on the north west direction of the great lake I would say ... yes
Int   ok of the great lake ok ... and
01   and you will be able to see me
Int   ok and that's it

8.4 Speaker 5: Happy event task (05-HE)

05   well I got a quite interesting childhood
Int   yes
05   because er I guess because I've got a lot of cousins
Int   cousin yes ah
05   yeah and I have a brother and many cousins
Int   uhuh
05   um of similar ages
Int   yes
05   so I remember that when we were young
Int   yeah
05   erm my parents used to take me to the Lantau island
Int   [di læntaʊ] mhm
05   yeah it's it's an island in Hong Kong
Int   mhm mhm
05   and like it's a tourist resort areas
Int   ok
05   something like that
Int   yeah yeah
05   so we used to go there every every week
Int   mhm
05   yeah so I learned how to cycle there
Int   oh
05   'cause 'cause Hong Kong is like um a very big city
Int   yeah yeah
05   very busy cities there's no way ((laugh)) you can cycle
Int   yes
05   is really dangerous unless if you go to er like Lantau island
Int   mhm

	05	New Territories
	Int	mhm
	05	then you've got a chance to do it
	Int	okay yeah
60	05	so when I was young my parents took me there er every week so my brother and I both learned cycling there
	Int	that's good yeah
	05	and it was so nice 'cause you would pass through er like country houses
	Int	mhm mhm
	05	yeah and j- I sometimes you could see the cow
	Int	oh really
	05	and
	Int	so it's really the countryside ((unintelligible))
	05	and and some dogs
	Int	uhuh
	05	yeah some horrible ones ((laughs))
	Int	ah horrible ((laughs))
	05	yeah ((laughs)) cause they barks a lot and
	Int	are you did were you afraid and yes
	05	yeah we were ya . . . but it was so funny cause I remember that we've got all sort of imagination when we were young
	Int	mhm mhm
	05	and my cousin and I and my brother er once went um to a river and caught some fish
	Int	yeah yeah
	05	they've got very tiny ones
	Int	mhm
	05	and then we got a fancy idea of using um um a plastic box
	Int	mhm
120	05	it should be um something um those um it's rubbish actually
	Int	yes
	05	ya but we like recycling it
	Int	yeah
	05	for the fish ((laughs))
	Int	and we caught the fish and put them there . . . and actually it's very nice it's like a house with rooms it's got partitions
	Int	uhuh
	05	so we put water in it
	Int	so was it like a a bucket or like a big box
	05	no it's not er it's probably something for I think um some toys

Int   uhuh uhuh
05   so sometimes when you got a box of toys and you took it out
Int   uhuh ok yeah
05   and then they put different things here and there
Int   mhm
05   so you've got something like partitions
Int   mhm
05   so we er put the fish
Int   that were the rooms of your house
05   yeah ((laughs))
Int   yes ((laughs))
05   so ((laughs)) we separated the fish into different areas
Int   yeah yeah
05   and then maybe because we were naughty or like when we caught er the fish maybe we hurt them or
Int   uhuh
05   some of them looked very sick
Int   oh yeah

180 05   so we move them ((laughs)) to one partition this is the sick room
Int   ((laughs))
05   ((laughs))
Int   yeah
05   yeah it was so funny actually and then I remember that . . . um my cousin they actually took a few back home cause we er all of us were not living in the Lantau island
Int   yes yes
05   yeah we just went there once a week
Int   yeah
05   it's like we've got a cottage or something like that there
Int   yeah
05   so
Int   you had a cottage there so you er
05   um
Int   a place to stay and everything
05   they my uncle's got one
Int   mhm mhm
05   so we use to go there a lot and then what happen was the fish er grew really really fast
Int   so you kept them in there in the this box or
05   well my em I think most of them like er at the end

Int   yeah

05   we let them go back home to the river (laugh)

Int   you mean at the end of the day or at the end of the summer

240 05   at the end of the day probably

Int   ok

05   and then but then . . . my cousin kept a few

Int   ok yeah

05   ya and took them home

Int   oh right yeah

05   and they fed them

Int   home to Hong Kong

05   ya it's also

Int   ah

05   in Hong Kong Lantau island is also in Hong Kong ((unintelligible))

Int   alright yeah ok

05   but he took them back to their home

Int   yes

05   ya and then um the fish grew really really fast

Int   ok yeah

05   ya and their mum was so angry

Int   ((laughs))

05   'cause I think at the beginning it was like that size

Int   oh right

05   and then and then it was like longer than my finger

Int   uhuh

05   it has grew really really fast

Int   ((laughs))

05   ((laughs)) but it's so horrible it . . . they they really didn't look like fish at all . . . it's very strange I don't know what they they are

Int   mhm

05   actually

Int   mhm mhm

05   yeah and then and . . . um the other time when we went back er

Int   yeah

05   we just er cause because their mother didn't like them a lot

Int   yeah

300 05   so they let them go back to the river

Int   didn't like to didn't like the fish yeah

05   no

Int   yeah

05   no but there were quite a lot of happy times

Int   yes yes

05   ya like we cycle at night

Int   uhuh good

05   and then once I didn't know my brother er who's in front of me

Int   yes yes

05   who's ahead of me he stopped his bike I didn't see it

Int   ah you didn't have enough light or

05   no

Int   no

05   no and then

Int   so what happened ((laughs))

05   so ((laughs)) my bike clashed with it

Int   ah

05   and then I fell off to the other side into the field

Int   into the field yeah ((laughs))

05   yeah ((laughs)) yeah

Int   so how how old were you at that time ((unintelligible))

05   I guess like five or six years old

Int   ((unintelligible))

05   yeah

Int   so that was forbidden anyway I guess get up during the night and then then so things like ((unintelligible))

05   well well my parents allowed us to go out

Int   they allowed you

05   I think my father came with us probably or my uncle came with us

Int   uhuh uhuh

360 05   yeah but I think it's quite interesting cause er nowadays usually parents won't allow you

Int   yes

05   to do all this kind of things

Int   yes yes

05   yeah but I still remember that in my childhood

Int   ((laughs))

05   I've got some k- some sort of experience of that

Int   yeah

05   yeah . . . so that was some very interesting time

Int   I guess so yeah

05   yeah

Int	so . . . you went there over the whole year during your weekends
05	I think . . . I think
Int	((unintelligible))
05	until I got to primary school
Int	ok
05	yeah and then we didn't go that often
Int	yeah
05	yeah because work becomes very busy
Int	yes yes
05	yeah . . . but I think it's very interesting maybe because of these kind of thing I was quite childish in a way
Int	mhm
05	((laughs)) 'cause erm like I actually didn't understand a lot of things that my classmate erm talk about
Int	mhm

420

05	because I used to study in a very prestigious school in Hong Kong
Int	ok yeah
05	and then a lot of them were very rich
Int	mhm
05	so um they . . . you wouldn't believe their life cause I remember that er em one of my neighbour s- th- um so the classmate sitting next to me
Int	yes yes
05	he ask me um ((name)) what do you usually order for food during you dinner time . . . so it's like in their family they had a practice that
Int	oh ((unintelligible))
05	oh like each of them order a food or . . . or like they took turns like today maybe
Int	because they went to to to have dinner in a restaurant
05	they didn't go out
Int	ok
05	they didn't out they didn't go out
Int	((unintelligible))
05	in their family they've got maids
Int	yes
05	yeah um probably some cook I don't know
Int	yes yes

05	and they used to had er have this idea of you know erm each of
480	them took a turn to order food something like that

Int	right yes
05	and I totally didn't understand
Int	((laughs))
05	what he said . . . what what do you mean
Int	yes
05	and then I think erm he said yesterday I order erm
Int	((laughs))
05	barbecue er . . . um pork something like that
Int	uhuh uhuh
05	roast pork
Int	uhuh
05	and then er but then in Chinese in Cantonese he em he used the term *mat6 zap1 caa1 siu1* but in my family we only say *caa1 siu1* every time
Int	mhm
05	every time we we won't describe the first part the first part
Int	uhuh
05	is about a barbecue sauce
Int	uhuh uhuh
05	the roasted one but my parents never said something like that
Int	uhuh
05	they they only say the pork
Int	yeah yeah
05	((unintelligible)) these two words so um in my mind I still remember that clearly cause in Cantonese we've got a lots of words with erm exactly the same sound same sounds but different meanings
Int	yeah
05	so that the first word *mat6* is similar er is actually the same sound as um the melon
Int	mhm . . . melon yes
05	that em cause you've got one kind of melon is green in colour when you cut it open it's light green
Int	yes yeah
05	yeah so that kind of melon
Int	uhuh
05	em it's exactly the same sound and then I was asking myself is it tasty with the the melon sauce
Int	so melon and the pig
05	and the pork
Int	the pork really yes
05	((laughs)) yeah I was thinking in that way

540

Int	mhm
05	I still remember that
Int	and you learnt the word later on and and and
05	but I didn't telled him cause I felt very embarrassed of you know not um knowing something that they said
Int	uhuh
05	I usually didn't say anything
Int	yeah yeah
05	but actually I didn't understand it until when I got older and I saw you know menus in restaurants
Int	yes yes
05	then I realised what that was
600 Int	mhm
05	yeah but I still remember that
Int	oh yeah that's ah that's quite funny yeah ((laughs))
05	yeah ((laughs))
Int	yeah
05	my brother and I used to be very naughty
Int	oh yes ((laughs))
05	but but I'm glad that I've got all these experience
Int	yes yes
05	yeah
Int	well you didn't tell us a naughty story really that all was
05	yeah I can tell you if you don't mind
Int	well go ahead
05	if you want to know
Int	yeah go ahead
05	I actually broke my forehead I injure it
Int	oh oh
05	when I was young
Int	yeah
05	and I got eleven stitches
Int	eleven stitches oh
05	yeah ((laughs))
Int	did that hurt a lot
05	em I couldn't remember I guess I was only three probably
Int	ok how did so how did you do it
05	I actually I cried a lot when I was a kid
Int	yeah yeah
05	so I went to the same kindergarden with my brother
Int	yes

660 05   he's my elder brother he's just one year older . . . so . . . erm . . .
         cause I cried a lot my teacher always took me to my brother's

Int   mhm

05   classroom and let me sit next to him

Int   yeah

05   and then I would stop crying

Int   ok

05   yeah that's the only way to stop me

Int   that's the only way

05   yeah so to get rid of me ((laughs)) and then erm but whenever I
     erm sat next to my brother

Int   mhm

05   I would become very er jumpy

Int   uhuh

05   as naughty as him

Int   mm

05   and then I remember once our teachers gave us some colouring
     book um I guess we had some

Int   mhm mhm

05   kind of art lesson

Int   yes yes

05   and then my what my brother did was he climbed out on his
     desk

Int   mhm mhm

05   and he jumped off

Int   er d- out of the window or

05   no no he's he's just er climb up and then jump er jumped

Int   to the floor yeah mhm mhm

05   and then I just follow cause

Int   uhuh

720 05   everything he did I would follow

Int   you just ((laughs))

05   whatever and my parents always laughed at me they said um
     your brother never got into trouble ((laughs))

Int   and you do ((laughs))

05   you were always the one getting in troubles

Int   ah

05   so I did the same thing and then I . . . I really didn't know why
     I really fell on the ((snorts)) on the floor and my forehead
     ((unintelligible))

Int   that's why you broke your oh

05	yeah
Int	oh god
05	yeah yeah
Int	((laughs))
05	((laughs)) and there were other times like
Int	((unintelligible))
05	in my home we've got erm beds
Int	yes yes
05	cause when we were young we live with our er grandfather
Int	ok yeah yeah
05	so he got a room my brother and I both live with my parents in one room
Int	uhuh
05	and then we've got a bed er for my brother
Int	yeah
05	and me and then my parents got their double bed
Int	yes yeah
05	and I we used to jump like that
Int	oh jump between the beds
05	yeah
Int	it must be fun yes

780	05	and then . . . my brother never got problem
	Int	but you did ((laughs))
	05	((laughs)) yeah I did ((laughs)) so . . . I I guess I I hurt er my leg
	Int	oh god
	05	yeah luckily it was not broken
	Int	yes yeah
	05	((laughs)) yeah but it's always happen like that
	Int	((laughs)) yeah jumping in bed I think that that's a very nice experience for all of us ((laughs))
	05	yeah my brother and I never er never never felt scared
	Int	uhuh uhuh
	05	of doing all sort of dangerous things
	Int	yeah yeah
	05	and we also have funny times like erm my cousin
	Int	yeah
	05	er two of them lived above us
	Int	mm
	05	so we use have dinner together every night
	Int	yeah
	05	and then after dinner erm er we would play together

	Int	yeah
	05	in my parents' room
	Int	mhm
	05	and then ah ((laughs)) cause we saw cartoons when we were young
	Int	mhm
840	05	and you know in cartoons you've got many ah imaginable stuff
	Int	yes
	05	something that never happen in real life
	Int	sure yeah yeah
	05	but we thought it could happen like um we saw like two trees
	Int	mhm
	05	I don't know what you call that em they er they have something hang on the trees and someone would sleep there
	Int	oh yes
	05	it's like a mat thing
	Int	yes like a mat
	05	yeah I don't know what
	Int	yes
	05	that's call
	Int	like not sure
	05	I don't even know in my language
	Int	ok yes
	05	cause we don't have that thing
	Int	yes
	05	and then we always thought that it's comfortable is very comfortable very interesting
	Int	yeah
	05	so what we did was
	Int	((laughs))
	05	((laughs)) we er use a blanket
	Int	yeah
	05	that we found in my parents' room
	Int	yes yeah
	05	oh and then ((breath)) like erm two of us erm carry each side on each end
	Int	yeah
	05	ok and then one of us
	Int	together with your cousins and
	05	yeah yeah
	Int	ok

	05	that's right
	Int	yeah
	05	and then we took turns
	Int	ok
900	05	so one of us would sleep there on on the blanket and then on each side we've got one person
	Int	yeah yeah
	05	there holding it out ((laughs))
	Int	((laughs))
	05	and then
	Int	it was funny
	05	it was so funny yeah
	Int	((laughs))

8.5 Speaker 5: Map task (05-MT)

	05	erm can you see a diamond mine next to you
	Int	yes there is a diamond mine yeah
	05	so you have to um … um … you have to face to the south
	Int	ok good yeah
	05	and then and then go straight
	Int	yep
	05	but don't go too far stick to the diamond mine
	Int	right yes
	05	yep then when you see the main entrance like you know like a building the main entrance 'cause it's it's a cave right
	Int	yes
	05	if you see that turn to your left
	Int	ok yeah
	05	yeah … and then so you you are now facing the east
	Int	yes
	05	right
	Int	yep
	05	so go straight
	Int	ok towards the east yes
	05	you should be able to see springboks
	Int	er no I don't see springboks no
	05	no you don't have springbok on your left
	Int	no I don't have the springboks there
60	05	ok so if you go further
	Int	yes

05   um can you see a highest view point

Int   yes there is one yes there's one . . . er well towards the north east direction of where I am standing

05   yeah that's right

Int   ok yeah

05   that's right so um . . . um the springboks actually is before the highest view point on your left

Int   ok good yeah

05   yeah ok

Int   so where shall I go now

05   and then um you should um go past the highest view point fr- from the back of it

Int   right so I

05   so

Int   so I pass on the

05   so

Int   on the west side and the north of it is that

05   um basically you have to go north after you pass the springboks

Int   yes

05   you have to um go to the north

Int   yes

05   so you can um go behind the highest view point

Int   ok

05   pass through it around it

Int   yes yes I

05   ok

120   Int   I can see I can get around that yes

05   and then you get around it and then you you you will get to the other side of the highest view point

Int   mhm

05   ok

Int   ok yes so I'm at the east side of the

05   yeah

Int   of the highest view point now

05   that's right and then now um you should be facing the south

Int   yes

05   and then um just um walk along

Int   mmm

05   just go ahead

Int   yeah

05   and then can you see um the safari truck in front of you

Int   yes that's ... so I come so I pass by the overgrown gully there and and there is the safari truck

05   yeah that's right

Int   is that right

05   yeah

Int   ok so what to do when I'm at the safari truck

05   yeah once you see that you can carry on to walk um towards your right hand side

Int   mhm

05   just go straight

Int   go towards the east then

05   um

Int   the west sorry

05   um yeah to the yeah that's right and then you can see um so just just pass through the erm safari truck

Int   mhm

180 05   and then um can you see a field station um ahead on the right on the right hand side

Int   oh there is a field station right at the very far the other's the other end of the

05   yeah

Int   of the territory that's quite far actually

05   oh

Int   there is one

05   ok well there's actually a closer one

Int   all right

05   instead of that one there's a closer one

Int   yes

05   can you can you see um ... a banana tree that is nearer to you

Int   yes yes there's a banana tree yes

05   yeah yep so just walk towards that direction

Int   uhuh uhuh

05   yeah ok

Int   yes yes good yeah

05   and then um you can so again you have to go around the banana tree

Int   right yes

05   yeah from from from behind and then and then um pass the banana tree and then go er south

Int   so I pass the banana tree on the west side and go south then yeah

240 05 yeah that's right and then just walk ahead until you see the gold mine

Int I don't have a gold mine on my map but

05 ok

Int if I if I walk ahead south well south from the banana tree there's a rock fall

05 ok that's not not so far

Int oh not so far as that ok mhm

05 you don't have to go ahead like that you um just go ahead and then um . . . you have to turn to your left . . . like from the banana tree

Int yes

05 if you go further south

Int yes

05 before you get to the rock fall don't don't get there

Int ok

05 there's still a- distant

Int ok

05 and then you turn to your left hand side

Int ok so between the banana tree and the rock fall

05 and go ahead

Int yeah

05 yeah and then and then can you see a rope bridge

Int yes I know where that is

05 yep

Int yes

05 yeah so you have to pass you you have to go past you you have to cross the bridge

Int mhm

05 so go ahead right d'you see that

300 Int ok I cross then I cross the rope bridge yeah that's fine

05 yep you cross it

Int I can see where that is yes

05 after you cross it um um you turn to the south again

Int oh right so

05 and go further south

Int just south of the rope bridge that's where the crocodiles are

05 ok um I don't have crocodiles here but I can see giraffes do you have giraffes there

Int oh yes the giraffes are further south

05 yeah that's right so go further south until

Int	ok so go past the crocodiles towards the giraffes yes
05	you pass the yeah until you pass the giraffes
Int	ok
05	yeah and you you don't want them to hurt you so so you have to walk past them
Int	ok yes
05	and then
Int	especially with the crocodiles
05	yeah that's right so um after you past the giraffes
Int	yes
05	and you can turn to your right
Int	ok
05	and then can you see a great lake very very far away
Int	yes I I can see where that is
05	so

360	Int	so I first pass by the dis- disused warehouse then come to the great lake then
	05	yeah so um er just walk towards the great lake um area just towards that just go straight
	Int	ok yeah
	05	yeah and then er walked along the side of the great lake
	Int	which which side are you
	05	um the the south the one that's south
	Int	the south the south part
	05	just alonged it
	Int	yes ok yeah yeah
	05	yeah and then . . . er after that you can see the finish point . . . on your right and you can see me there
	Int	after the great lake on the right so up again towards the north
	05	yeah that's right
	Int	ok that's where you are
	05	there you can see me yeah
	Int	well thank you very much

8.6 Speaker 8: Happy event task (08-HE)

08	well ((unintelligible)) let me talk about my trip to Canada
Int	your trip to Canada
08	yes
Int	yes
08	I went there last year in the summer holiday

Int   aha aha

08   and because my sister she was living she is actually she's there now she's living in Edmonton a little town in Canada

Int   yes

08   and I went there to visit her

Int   aha

08   because at that time it was after graduation so I've got about three months' holiday

Int   aha aha

08   um on the first day when I was in Canada I did not go straightly to Edmonton instead I stayed in Vancouver

Int   mhm

08   and my sister came from Edmonton to Vancouver to meet me up

Int   right

08   and we . . . spent about four days there because I've never been to Vancouver before

Int   mhm

60 08   and . . . she took me to many places and I enjoyed the four days because . . . Vancouver is actually quite different from Edmonton

Int   uhuh

08   Vancouver they have high-rise buildings they have . . . relatively good food

Int   yeah

08   and there are a lot of national parks and beaches and you will never found it in Edmonton

Int   ok

08   because Edmonton is a place er like in the mainland area but Vancouver is along the coast line

Int   yes yes

08   ((breath)) ah what's in- what was interesting is that at that time I knew that . . . Vancouver has . . . a place to breed salmon because

Int   mhm

08   before that I didn't know that but . . . er I was not lucky enough because I didn't have a chance to try the salmon there

Int   yeah

120 08   after that we took a flight back to Edmonton . . . but at that time my sister ha- had to go back to work

Int   yeah

08   so mostly I spent my time on my own sometimes I would go to the shopping malls . . . some museums

Int   yeah

08   or some sight-seeing spots but er it was not that good because I was on my own

Int   yeah

08   every time when my sister er finished her work . . . she would join me and we would go to some restaurants or other sight-seeing spots

Int   yeah

08   to have fun

Int   mhm

08   em actually she she she was very good because I know that she was very tired after work for like eight to ten hours every day . . . but she would take me to many places . . . and we just enjoyed our days in Edmonton

180 Int   mhm mhm

08   sometimes she would even took me to the park to have roller blade . . . um skating

Int   yes

08   and oh sometimes we would go shopping together and have food because both of us love eating food

Int   mhm

08   a lot

Int   ((laughs))

08   we went to many places many restaurants to have food

Int   mhm what kind of food is that

08   well there were a lot we have sushi . . . seafood . . . pasta

Int   mhm

08   steak . . . er bakeries we love bakeries a lot

Int   aha

08   chocolates desserts

Int   aha

08   all the food that we love but sometimes we wanted to save money so we went to the supermarket to get a lot of raw food and we go we went back home to cook

Int   uhuh mhm

240 08   mhm . . . ah she was not good at cooking because . . . she said that she does not have any time to cook

Int   mhm

08   so erm usually erm the cook I was the cook

Int   aha aha
08   the cook for her um . . . we really had fun there
Int   mhm
08   yes I enjoyed that month in Edmonton and also in Vancouver
Int   yeah
08   but time flew and I had to come back go back to Hong Kong
Int   yes yeah yes
08   mhm
Int   so you spent one month there
08   yes I was there for a month
Int   mhm
08   mhm
Int   and do you usually er live in Hong I mean now you live in England but
08   yes I stayed in Hong Kong actually for my life before I came here
Int   right mhm
08   mhm
Int   and your sister did she live in Hong Kong or . . . did she is she in Canada just temporarily
08   um oh erm she . . . she's there for like forever
Int   ok
08   mhm she went there nine years ago
Int   ok yeah

300 08   and finished her degree and she is now working there
Int   ok
08   mhm
Int   yeah yeah and was it the first time you visited your sister in Canada
08   mm . . . well . . . if my memory serves me well it should be in 2004 . . . four years ago . . . and then I went there again last year
Int   yes
08   yeah
Int   so the second time
08   yes it it it was the second time
Int   ok yeah
08   mhm but at time I stayed in calgary instead of Edmonton because at that time she was working in Calgary . . . mhm
Int   yeah yeah
08   mhm
Int   ok well thanks very much
08   yes

8.7 Speaker 8: Map task (08-MT)

08	mmm first you have to go north and on your left hand side you will see a diamond mine
Int	er nor- ... by north you mean now er just to get is north for you down
08	yeah yeah
Int	ok
08	er should I
Int	that's fine
08	((laughs))
Int	I mean on other maps sometimes most of the time north is
08	oh south
Int	south ok all right
08	did I say north
Int	i i thought you said north
08	sorry
Int	ok so north south east west yeah
08	yeah yeah yeah
Int	yeah right I go south then
08	yeah ah you go south um you will see a diamond mine on your left hand side did you see it
Int	yes yes yes I know where that is I can see that
08	ok and then ... when you see the diamond mine you have to turn to the east
Int	mhm
08	and walk straight
Int	straight oh eh straight yeah
08	yes and then at the point where you see a springboks

60

Int	oh right yeah
08	do you see it
Int	no I don't know where the springboks are if I walk if I pass the diamond mine and walk straight ahead I eventually I get to an overgrown gully ... erm
08	ok er is it on your east side
Int	that's that's the right and the east of the map
08	all right and round uh
Int	below the highest view point
08	oh yeah you're right ... at that point you have to turn north
Int	mhm
08	and then you will be walking towards the highest view point

Int   ok yes
08   yes
Int   I can see that
08   and then you will go past that view point
Int   mhm
08   and just like you are going to the east
Int   ok
08   after that after you have passed the view point you will be going south
Int   mmm
08   and then walk straight
Int   ok yeah
08   and at the end of that road you will see a safari truck

120 Int   ok I can see where that is
08   can you see that
Int   yes yes
08   yeah lovely and then go to the . . . east west side er west east side
Int   west
08   no west south south side
Int   south west
08   yes
Int   yes
08   south west and at the end of that road you will see a field station
Int   ok er south west of the safari truck you say
08   yeah exactly
Int   I see a banana tree south west
08   yes
Int   but quite far away
08   exactly just go that way
Int   ok yeah
08   mhm . . . and then you will uhm follow that road and you will see the banana tree and then just follow that road because . . . after you have gone south west you will go . . . to the west direction
Int   mhm
08   and then at the end of that road please turn south and cross that banana tree
Int   all right after the banana tree I go south yes
08   yes after that
Int   mhm

180 08   at the end of that road you will see a gold mine
    Int   ok after the banana tree south if I continue going sou- I don't
          see a gold mine on my map but I can see a rock fall south of the
          banana tree
    08   oh exactly
    Int   but that's quite far away
    08   yes quite far away but er doesn't matter er just you will go . . .
          south and not exactly to the rock fall . . . and then suppose you
          will see a gold mine and then at some point you will see a rope
          bridge on the east
    Int   so where do you have to go erm
    08   it's quite far away
    Int   from the gold mine
    08   from the gold mine go east
    Int   east ok
    08   yes east and then
    Int   all right and there is a rope bridge yes I can see that
    08   yes cross that bridge . . . cross the bridge and then go south
    Int   ok yeah
    08   and you will see a group a group of giraffes and they are quite far
          away but just go that way

240 Int   I see where that is yes
    08   and go through the gira- giraffes and go to the west side
    Int   ok yeah
    08   and then you will just follow that road . . . and then turn south
    Int   west and then south
    08   yes
    Int   so there is after the giraffes there is a disused warehouse
    08   but ah do you see a great lake
    Int   and afterwards there is a great lake yeah
    08   yes follow that road and go through the great lake and I will be
          at the end of that road
    Int   ok so I go south of the great lake
    08   now you go south and then you go west
    Int   ok
    08   and you will see the great lake on your right hand side
    Int   ok yeah
    08   and then turn a little bit north and I will be there
    Int   and that's where you are
    08   yes
    Int   ok thanks very much

8.8 Speaker 9: Happy event task (09-HE)

09   yes I I think is about going to a wild camp with some of my friends
Int   aha yes
09   yes so it's around when I was ah fifteen years old
Int   fifteen years
09   yes I I . . . because my mothers er he he er my mother she has a er some friends who go to church regularly
Int   mhm
09   and the church organise a a wild camp activities . . . so um
Int   wild camp or isn't it
09   wild wild camp yes
Int   aha
09   and my sisters and my mother we we join the wild camp
Int   yes
09   it's the first time we go to camping but not go to but not going to like a hotel
Int   yes
09   or other er more . . . um more better facilities
Int   yeah

09   camp side so that's why I was very excited but um . . . it it takes so much time to arrive to the camp camp site um and then I think
60   it takes er . . . it tooks er more than an hour travel by bus
Int   mhm
09   and than we had to walk for another two hours
Int   aha yeah
09   yes while we arrive we can see a very beautiful environment
Int   yes
09   yes um but the funny thing is there lots of um um cows' faeces
Int   cows yeah
09   the the cows' faeces which is very smelly
Int   aha yeah
09   aha and um but it it's ok um and then er . . . at the at the night we set of some camp fire we have barbecue
Int   mhm
09   and we sing together with some of the friends
Int   oh yeah
09   and we go to fishing at nights because at the night time is the best time for fishing
Int   mhm

09	the the fish they are not very sensitive to the shining hook
Int	yeah
09	yes er and ... after the night time on the other day we have some mass game

120	Int	aha
	09	so we we play with other people
	Int	Yeah
	09	and it's some kind of competitions and
	Int	ok
	09	some people win some some lose and ... er so after several hours so it's around noon time and then we have to go back so we walk another two hours and then one hour bus and ... came back to the city
	Int	yeah yeah
	09	aha
	Int	so er all in all you stayed how how long did you stay there er
	09	um I I just stay there for one night
	Int	just one night aha yeah
	09	yes aha
	Int	ok and how many how many people were there
	09	um
	Int	was it a big camp
	09	ah I think there are in total fifty people
	Int	ah quite ((unintelligible))
	09	yes and then five people in one tent so there are ten tents set up
	Int	aha aha
	09	um on the on the camp site
	Int	yes
	09	yes any more er
	Int	so all of them just went for one night
	09	yes
	Int	ok yeah
	09	aha
	Int	that's ((unintelligible))

180	09	but I saw some other people but not in our group
	Int	yes
	09	they they go to I think they stay more than one one night and they are more well equipped
	Int	mhm
	09	and ... um ... I think they stay one night at at this camp side and move to another camp side

Int yeah

09   the day after

Int aha aha

09   yes

Int aha

09   aha

Int so were you . . . were you alone I mean er with other kids

09   aha

Int or were you was your mother with you

09   oh yes my mother

Int ((unintelligible))

09   yes my mother is always with me because I am fifteen and my mother is very worry if I I wa- was lost

Int ok

09   in forest

Int ok aha so all of the kids had their parents with them or their mothers at least

09   um yes both bo- all of the children they are still very young . . . I think I am one of the older

Int ok

09   yeah

Int yeah

09   and then um . . . every children they they came with their parents and actually each tents um is a unit for a family

240

Int ok

09   yes um so we have like ten family

Int aha yes

09   aha yes aha

Int so and all in all they were fifty people not fifty kids

09   oh yeah yeah

Int alright yeah ok

09   but it's a very a lovely experience for me

Int yes

09   because after this I I never do any wild camp any

Int ok

09   any more aha

Int did you love going out to to I don't know I don't know into the nature for walks or is that

09   yes

Int I don't know how easy that is

09   aha

Int	but
09	I think I quite enjoy it
Int	yes
09	but the fact is um so people is always peoples are always afraid of mosquito some insects
Int	ok yeah
09	or even snake er because
Int	snakes or
09	snakes yeah
Int	aha yeah
09	snakes er ... yes ... um and I think people do not want to bother too many thing because
Int	yes
09	you have to get all the equipments
09	yeah
09	and travel fo- for a long way
Int	it's not very comfortable is it
09	yeah aha

300	Int	it's like an adventure
	09	yeah
	Int	yeah
	09	and sometimes you you may get lost or the worst thing is there maybe some thief so they they try to rob you
	Int	oh
	09	some robber
	Int	oh robbers ah
	09	yeah
	Int	it that happened to you
	09	so it sounds quite scary
	Int	yeah
	09	in a sense yeah
	Int	yeah
	09	aha
	Int	and how far from the Hong Kong would that be be did normally did you live in the city of Hong Kong itself
	09	yes um actually Hong Kong is very small
	Int	alright
	09	yes and ... but we ... er actually the geography Hong Kong is there are more urban area there more there are more rural area than than urban area
	Int	ok

09   yes but um if you go to very er very deep into a forest

Int mhm

09   I I'm not sure if is if is good to call a forest so but e- but there are lot of trees

Int yeah

09   er very tall but not like a not like a um tropical rain forest

Int yeah

360 09 er but it it still take like three to four hours to to go there . . . aha

Int yeah yeah

09   but the fact is er maybe because Hong Kong is small or we have too many people

Int mhm

09   so even you go very away from the cities you still find a lot of people

Int yes

09   still around you so is is good that you feel some kind of safety

Int ok

09   but on the other hand you may think we are still in the city

Int yeah

09   but the context is different

Int yeah

09   aha

Int aha

09   yeah

Int so when you go into the nature you are not alone

09   aha

Int actually ((laughs))

09   yes we are not alone

Int yeah

09   and sometimes is quite noisy

Int ok ((laughs))

09   yeah as I as I tell told you er so we played the mass game

Int yeah

09   so at the same actually we we create a lots of noise

Int yeah

09   aha it may disturb other people

Int mhm

09   aha but on the other hand they are oth- other people who do the same things ((laughs))

Int yeah yeah

09	so actually we just bring the the city life to the
Int	((laughs))
09	to to the rural area ((laughs)) aha
Int	yeah yeah
09	aha

420 Int yeah so that was the only time you did you were went on a camping trip really

09	yes aha the next time I do not go this kind of wild camp but
Int	yes
09	just go to er a vacation centre or resort centre
Int	yes yes
09	ah . . . because they're well equipped they have prepare all the faci- they pro they provides all the facilities like showering
Int	yeah
09	er er and like sport game
Int	yeah yeah
09	yes which is easy and we do not have to plan too much ah in
Int	mhm
09	advance and the the the because it's um . . . subsidise by the government
Int	mhm
09	so the entrance fee and the food are relatively cheap
Int	ok yeah
09	and the hygiene quality ah the hygiene and all the conditions is is very nice
Int	yes
09	yeah and there are more than one er this kind of centre in Hong Kong so we we can try different one
Int	mhm mhm
09	but not getting bored by any one of these
Int	yes yes

480 09 yes

Int	yes
09	so I so later I more enjoy doing this rather than going er a wild camp but I I do do a lot of hiking
Int	ok yeah
09	yeah so it's less physically demand and after like six hours' walk I can go back to my home and have
Int	yeah
09	a proper shower
Int	yeah yeah

09   and have a proper meal with my friends

Int   aha aha

09   aha yes ... but I I think in general Hong Kong people they they love to go to the .. to see the nature because our city life is quite ... quite high tech and ... busy so

Int   yes

09   we need some fresh air

Int   yes yes

09   er especially ... the weather in Hong Kong is quite hot so we always kept in a air con room

Int   yeah

09   and

Int   yeah is it like tropical or

09   er yes I think it's tropical or subtropical or is always very humid

Int   yes yes

09   yes and hot aha

Int   aha

09   and because it's so small

Int   yeah

09   it's a bit noisy

Int   mhm

540   09   so if you don't keep yourself in the air con room you m- you will possibly be disturbed by the traffic's noise

Int   oh you can't just open the windows ((laughs))

09   yes is impossible

Int   yes

09   aha if you want to concentrate aha

Int   yeah yeah

09   aha

8.9 Speaker 9: Map task (09-MT)

09   um so we are at the starting point and do you see a diamond mine

Int   yeah oh sorry you can use terms like south and north or east or west

09   aha

Int   or left and right

09   I see if it's easier

09   I see um

Int   yeah I see the diamond mine yep

	09	yes you see so um now go south until you pass the diamond mine
	Int	ok yeah
	09	and then you turn to er then you go east until you see a springboks
	Int	right I go east I don't see where the springboks are
	09	aha
	Int	if I go east until the end of the the territory here
	09	yes
	Int	I come to an overgrown gully is that does that mean anything to you
	09	um ... so do you see there's a very high mountain
	Int	yes there is a highest view point yep
60	09	I see so um ... so you keep going east ... um and then um but ... do not pass the the mountain but you go you keep going
	Int	mhm
	09	I think before you you arrive to the mountain you will see the springboks
	Int	right
	09	um so if you see a springboks pass through it and then go north and then
	Int	north yeah
	09	yeah and then you will you will be ah at the foot of the mountain and then you keep going north and just um when you see ... ah you you pass the mountain and then you turn east again
	Int	ok yeah
	09	so after you pass the whole mountain go down and you try to look for safari truck
	Int	ok yeah I can see one of those yeah
120	09	ok so if you arrive the safari truck you go um a bit er ... south west
	Int	south west
	09	yes um
	Int	do you pass by the safari truck is it do you pass it south or north
	09	um ... er pass the south
	Int	mm
	09	and then you will possibly see a field station
	Int	ok I don't see a f- well there is one field station which is at the opposite of
	09	mhm
	Int	of the map really
	09	I see so um ...

Int   it's the only one I can see

09   ok so you you see the one er which is nearer to the safari truck
      . . . er safari truck

Int   mhm

09   yeah so ah . . . so if you see this field station you keep going and
      I guess you possibly see a banana tree

Int   ok yeah I see I I I see where the banana tree is

09   yeah but don't go too far away from the banana tree where you'll
      see another field station so ah while you you saw the banana tree
      go south again

Int   ok yeah

09   and look for a gold mine er

180 Int   a gold mine I don't see a gold mine

09   mhm

Int   but if I go south

09   yes

Int   from the banana tree there is a rock fall

09   I see actually the gold mine is er . . . at the midway of banana tree
      and rock fill

Int   ok

09   rock fall

Int   ok yeah

09   so you go down and you see a gold mine and then you go east
      again

Int   mhm mhm

09   until you see the rope bridge

Int   ok yes I can see where that is

09   and cross the rope bridge

Int   yes

09   and then go south

Int   then go south

09   yes and you see . . . there there will be giraffe

Int   yes I can see where that is yeah

09   and then go west again

Int   and now west again after the giraffes yeah

09   yes and you possibly see rock fall and a great lake

Int   yes

09   but don't go to the rock fall

Int   yeah

09   but er go to the next side and then keep going

Int   mm

240　09　and then you go a bit north then I I think you can reach the finish point

Int　ok great past the great lake and then north again

09　mhm

Int　and that's where you are

09　yes

Int　ok

09　aha

Int　thanks very much

8.10 Speaker 10: Happy event task (10-HE)

10　when I was young erm I liked to go to er some places with my father

Int　mhm

10　at weekend and my father bring er brought me to er some amusement park

Int　amusement park yeah

10　yeah and there's one quite near to my house

Int　mhm

10　so my father dri- drove me to there and that amusement park was called . . . Lee Yuen . . . Lee Yuen

Int　mhm yeah

10　er but it was removed now so it's no longer here so at that time I went there and . . . actually I went there with my brother and my father and we enjoyed our time there like we play some games

Int　yes

10　and we play some er . . . small scale rides there for children rides

Int　small scale

10　rise

Int　rides

10　the rides the rides yeah for children's the ones

Int　yeah

60　10　so they are in a very small scales and yeah and also we . . . we n- normally stay there for a whole day

Int　mhm

10　and we enjoyed our time there

Int　did you go there often er

10　um I think around . . . once a month or once every two months because it's very close to my home

Int　yes yeah

10   yeah

Int   so you played with er small scale

10   the rides ... the rides

Int   what what is that er

10   so er there are some like er ... pirate ship er pirate

Int   ok

10   boat

Int   ok things like that

10   but they are very small scale one for children

Int   mhm yeah yeah and how long did you stay there the whole

10   for for whole day

Int   for the whole day

10   yeah every time

Int   yeah a um about what age were you at that time

10   oh at that time I think I was around eight years

Int   around eight years

10   years old

Int   is your brother er

10   young

Int   older or younger

10   younger than me

Int   younger than you

120 10   so at that time he was around three years old

Int   ok so did you take care of your brother then um um on the pirate ship or ((laughs))

10   yeah yeah

Int   yes

10   yeah yeah yeah

Int   ok and so you just went with your father

10   yeah

Int   there

10   father and my brother sometime my mothers go but not every time

Int   oh she didn't like going there

10   yeah ((laughs))

Int   no

10   not not not quite yeah

Int   mhm ... ok how big how big is is such an amusement park or how big was that amusement park

10   er it was a small one

Int   yeah

	10	there's another big one that's called Ocean Park
	Int	yeah
	10	which is still here in Hong Kong and . . . but in that er amusement park there were some animals
	Int	yeah
	10	so er it is famous for having an elephant there
	Int	an elephant
	10	mhm
	Int	yeah
	10	so we can feed it with the banana
	Int	oh right yeah
	10	mhm
	Int	is it a bit like a zoo then as well
	10	yeah quite like a zoo
	Int	aha aha
	10	mhm
180	Int	and what what other animals you see there . . . elephant or I mean what of kind animals are there
	10	well I forgot about them
	Int	yeah ((unintelligible))
	10	but as I remember there should be some . . . some horses
	Int	horses aha
	10	y- ya I think so
	Int	so you enjoyed the the pirate ship
	10	yeah yeah
	Int	and that kind of thing yeah
	10	yeah
	Int	that's where you spent most of your
	10	and also seeing the elephant every time I I feed fed it
	Int	ok
	10	with the em ba- banana
	Int	yeah so weren't scared at all of the elephant
	10	um not not really because is some kind of domestic elephant
	Int	yeah
	10	it's not wild
	Int	mm
	10	so it's very well behaved
	Int	yeah yeah yeah did your friends go there as well
	10	um not that time
	Int	mhm
	10	because er my father er it's it's that we had two of us so fath- my

father can only take care of two of us can not like go with many
young kids because it's too dangerous

Int   yes yeah

8.11 Speaker 10: Map task (10-MT)

10   in front of you can you see the diamond mine
Int   yes I can see the diamond mine yep
10   yeah please pass through it
Int   mhm
10   and then later on can you see the springboks
Int   right I pass on on which side of the diamond mine
10   ah actually if you keep walking straight you can see the springboks
Int   ok
10   can you see them
Int   after the dia- on the east of the diamond at the east side of the
       diamond mine
10   ah
Int   yeah
10   you can ah I see maybe you are at the corner um . . . try to turn
       left
Int   ok
10   and walk straight
Int   right
10   can you see the springboks
Int   I can't see springboks on my map but if I walk . . . if I walk straight
       ahead until the end of the map there is an overgrown gully
10   mmm
Int   to which I come . . . so is that where the springboks are
10   ah I'm not quite sure because I cannot see it in my map
Int   mhm

60 10   but maybe you try to keep going straight and can you see . . . the
           highest view point
    Int   yes there is the highest view point
    10   that's great so keep going at that in that di- direction
    Int   ok yeah yeah
    10   and so after you pass through the highest view point
    Int   ok yes
    10   um . . . can you see the safari tru- truck
    Int   right so I go round the highest view point then south again there
           is a safari truck yes

10	yeah
Int	I can see that yeah
10	mm and then keep going and ... on your right you should see the field sta- station can you see it
Int	there is a field sta- that's left of the safari truck then
10	mmm
Int	is that right
10	is it on the right
Int	on the west west side of the safari truck
10	yeah yeah so
Int	right but there's a field station right at the other end of the of the map ... at the extreme west really

120 10 oh extreme west ... oh I see yeah that's that's too far away
Int ok
10 there should be another one that's closer to you
Int between the field the other field station and the safari truck
10 yeah
Int is that
10 it's in between
Int mhm
10 yeah so ah please keep going to that direction
Int ok
10 and then ... um ... on your left hand side
Int yes
10 you can see a banana tree ... can you see it
Int right down there is a banana tree yes
10 mm
Int yup
10 and
Int so it should be on my left I have to walk
10 yeah you should turn left
Int aha
10 keep going and you will see the banana tree on your left
Int ok
10 and also yeah and after that please ... keep going and you can see another gold mine gold mine on your left
Int a gold mine on my left
10 yeah it should be at the corner

180 Int I don't have a gold mine on my map but if I turn south after the banana tree there is a rock fall
10 mmm rock fall

Int as well

10   mmm I cannot see it on my map . . . but can you see the . . . rope bridge

Int oh that's over there yes that's

10   it's a bit far away

Int kind of south east of the banana tree there's a rope bridge

10   yeah

Int yeah

10   yeah

Int mhm

10   so please ah cross that bridge

Int ok yeah

10   and . . . in the south you should see some giraffes can you see them

Int yes and there are giraffes yes

10   yeah

Int south of the rope bridge

10   please pass through them

Int mhm

10   and keep going

Int ok

10   and can you see the great lake

Int and there is the great lake yes

10   yeah please . . . keep going keep going

Int yeah

10   and then um . . . in the in in the direction of north of you

240 Int right on which side do I have to pass the great lake north or south

10   um the great lake should be on your right

Int ok

10   yeah so please keep going in that direction

Int mhm

10   and turn left er turn right

Int and then right again yeah

10   yeah

Int and that's where you are

10   and that's yeah that's where I am

Int thanks very much

10   thank you

Int thank you

Index

NB: Page numbers in *italics* refer to figures, maps and tables.